Penguin Education

KT-599-470

Adults Learning
Jennifer Rogers

Adults Learning
Jennifer Rogers

Penguin Books

Penguin Books Ltd, Harmondsworth,
Middlesex, England
Penguin Books Inc., 7110 Ambassador Road,
Baltimore, Md 21207, U.S.A.
Penguin Books Australia Ltd,
Ringwood, Victoria, Australia

First published 1971
Copyright © Jennifer Rogers, 1971

Made and printed in Great Britain by
Hazell Watson & Viney Ltd,
Aylesbury, Bucks
Set in Intertype Plantin

Contents

Introduction

This book is addressed to people who teach adults. It is about the basic factors that operate in adult classes, whether the teacher is an instructor or training officer in industry, a lecturer on a management course, a Workers' Educational Association tutor, or a teacher in an evening institute or technical college.

Many of the people who teach adults in these situations are unaware that they have anything in common. Their different organizations may be jealous of their own status and special interests. To some teachers, the content of what is to be taught may seem more important than an examination of whether there are methods which are generally appropriate to all adult learning.

It is true that there are many ways in which the subject itself dictates the methods, but this book does not and could not go into the special problems of teaching adults philosophy, mandarin Chinese or felt-slipper-making. Instead, it tries to suggest that the art of teaching adults is a broadly based and flexible one, whose principles can be applied and adapted to a wide variety of teaching situations.

There is no attempt to offer any easy, infallible guides to 'good' teaching. Research on adult learning is still pitifully thin in quantity and quality. Even if it were not, teaching and learning are such infinitely variable processes that different students, classes and teachers would continue to have particular needs which only they could interpret. The suggestions made about methods, approaches and materials are meant to outline a range of possibilities from which teacher and class can choose, rather than a set of rules which must be adhered to.

The first five chapters are about adult students: who they are, what brings them to classes, how they feel in a classroom, how they react to different teaching techniques, how they learn most easily, how they behave in groups, and with what sorts of teachers and teaching methods they are likely to feel happiest.

The second half of the book is about the practicalities: the advantages and disadvantages of carrying out particular teaching strategies such as 'discovery learning', programmed instruction, case studies or projects. These chapters also deal with problems such as the planning of resources, finding ways of giving individual attention to students in classes of widely spaced ability, and creating active, lively methods of learning.

One of the difficulties about teaching is its isolation. Teachers only rarely see, or are seen by, other teachers in action. They are largely protected by the awe, politeness or simply the indifference of their classes from knowing how students really assess their teaching. As one class member, quoted later in the book (p. 141), said of a hard-working, conscientious but incompetent teacher, 'It was less trouble to leave the class than to explain to him that he was going about fifty times too fast.'

This is why, throughout the book, I have illustrated certain points by direct quotation, where teachers and students of varied backgrounds and subjects describe their classroom experiences and speak for themselves. The quotes were solicited in an entirely *ad hoc* and non-sociological manner. Many friends and professional acquaintances generously wrote pieces themselves, and also collected an enormous amount of material for me from their students and colleagues. Most of these accounts were lengthy and absorbing, and it has only been possible to quote a few paragraphs from them. Others were written as notes and have been reconstructed as accurately as possible in continuous form. Some are verbatim descriptions taken down on tape or by hand. Since most of them are frank and some of them blunt, identifying details have been changed where necessary.

The book assumes a little, but not much, teaching experience. It also assumes that the word 'he' stands for 'he or she', and that 'tutor', 'training officer' and 'lecturer' are interchangeable with the word 'teacher', according to the context under discussion.

Finally, I must thank the innumerable friends and colleagues who gave me so much advice, help and encouragement. There are too many of them to thank individually here. I must, however, particularly thank Dr Michael Apter of the University College of South Wales and Monmouthshire, Dr Meredith

Belbin, Elizabeth Broughton of Leicestershire Education Authority, Leslie Chidgey of Sittingbourne College of Education, William Hampton and Michael Barratt-Brown of Sheffield University Extra-Mural Department, Brian Harris of the BBC, Cathal Mullan of Aer Lingus, Richard Silburn and Ken Coates of Nottingham University Extra-Mural Department, and Pat Tansey of Bulmershe College of Education, all of whom went to some trouble for me by arranging visits to their classes or by lending interesting material.

Four people were more closely concerned with the whole book. My secretary, Viv Morris, not only coped beautifully with an extraordinarily untidy manuscript, but also offered much cogent comment in the light of her own experience as an adult student and new teacher. Brian Groombridge read the first part of the book at an early stage and made many invaluable and detailed suggestions both on what was already written and on what was still to come. Professor Roy Shaw was a useful sounding-board at first-draft stage. My husband, Alan Rogers, was, as ever, a continuing source of constructive criticism and encouragement. His help and support were crucial. Remaining errors and omissions are, of course, entirely my responsibility.

Chapter I
Adult Students

Why they come

Adult educationists responsible for planning courses and programmes often torment themselves with the difficulty of fathoming the motives of students. They feel that if only they could be more definite about why some students come into adult education then they might be able to draw in many more with greater certainty, instead of waiting for the annual lottery of enrolment week, anxiously watching for what 'takes' and what doesn't, grieving over what might have 'taken' if only it had been included.

This guessing game is not so much the individual teacher's problem. But the teacher *should* be concerned with understanding the motives of his students. If he identifies some of the reasons which have brought each student into his class, this will provide a valuable first point of contact, and also give him access to a most powerful stimulus to learning.

The public image of adult education is full of unfavourable clichés, not the least of which is the idea that students come into adult education for disreputable motives. Sometimes these views are held just as strongly by the teachers as by those outside:

Only one thing brings adults to classes: the prospect of having a pleasant social evening at the expense of the local authority.

They come 90 per cent because they get a half day off work and they say that a respite from heavy labouring is worth it, even if it is education. The other reason they come is that they want to know enough about industrial relations to outwit management. It amuses some of the more left-wing brothers to think that management is actually paying for them to be here. It's an added piquancy, if you like.

In rebutting this sort of argument it is hard to know exactly what to put in its place, since remarkably little is known about the motives of adults in joining classes. Some local surveys have been made, and there has been one notable national one recently conducted by the National Institute of Adult Education into motivation and adequacy of provision; but all these can and do only skim the surface.*

Adults do not have only one motive for joining a class. In talking to an interviewer they may be reluctant to single out one reason as more important than another; they may even wish to hide a motive of which they think an interviewer might disapprove. This would particularly apply to inquiries made by evening institutes among their own students, who might well believe that the institute was only interested in hearing educationally respectable reasons for joining a class. It is hardly surprising then that in many of the local surveys prim reasons such as 'sheer love of the subject' tend to come out on top.

A further problem is that the students themselves may be unaware of some of their real motives. For instance, a man who comes to a class which he hopes will help him win promotion at work might also be interested in finding a captive audience for his political views. Though his apparent motive might be vocational, he might subconsciously be equally attracted by the opportunity to dominate and control other students. A woman who claims that her motive is to try to make friends may also unconsciously be searching for ideas and knowledge which will help her make sense of her world.

More fundamentally even than this, one might say that all such motives are superficial and that the only basic motive of every adult student is the need for achievement and reward, the need to feel 'good' at something. In practice, of course, motives are irretrievably mixed and attempts to sort out one from another are bound to be artificial, not only for the reasons already mentioned, but also because motives will vary from one area to another and from one type of institution to another. It is with these provisos in mind that the following analysis should be read.

Vocational motives

One of the most important single reasons for undertaking further education at all, particularly for young men, appears to be the *vocational* one that it might improve prospects of promotion and help in other ways at work. Even in that part of the National Institute of Adult Education (NIAE) survey based on students

*NIAE, 'Adequacy of provision', *Adult Education*, vol. 42, no. 6, 1970.

attending entirely non-vocational classes, nearly 10 per cent of the students said that their main motive was a vocational one. In a larger sample from the whole population the proportion shot up to over a third. Obviously in industrially or professionally based courses this motive will predominate to such an extent that it probably excludes all others. But in most other kinds of adult education or industrial training, what appears to be a straightforward vocational reason is frequently overlaid with other motives, such as being interested in the subject for its own sake or wanting to find some relief from boring and repetitive work. Even in the so-called 'leisure' classes there may be a vocational element.

I joined the silversmithing class partly because I've always been interested in this type of craft, but my main reason was that I was looking for a skill I could use to make some money while the children were young and which I could develop later into a full-time job.

I know it's not a formal qualification in the usual way, but I need the discipline of a long course and the vigour of an intellectual like Mr — to feel that I am really exploiting my interest in ecology. I hope to use what I learn here to teach my fifth form next year.

The university is conducting ten evening seminars on industrial relations. I've joined the course because the whole subject fascinates me. As a new shop steward I'm also hoping to pick up the sort of knowledge which will help me at work in negotiations with management.

We were offered the chance to train to use the new machines at the — plant. I put my name down straight away. The course included something on very elementary computer work and this is something I have always been meaning to find out more about.

Self-development

As these extracts show, the whole vocational area of motives often blurs imperceptibly into motives which can be roughly grouped together as self-development or personal enrichment. These might include the wish to improve one's general education, or a desire to pursue an interest in a particular subject or creative hobby. Most surveys show that self-development is far and away the most common reason students give for joining a class; indeed in the NIAE survey, over 40 per cent of the students, more of them women than men, thought that this had been their main motive. 'Self-development' is a vague phrase, but some of the ways in which students interpret it can be seen in the following extracts:

I decided it was time I attempted to pull together some of the heart-aches and pleasures of my sixty-two years. I hoped the philosophy classes could show me how other people had found an integrated system which could explain some of life's puzzling mysteries.

My chief reason for attending evening classes is that I have an insatiable desire to learn, even though I am now too old for any specialist knowledge to be of any material benefit financially.

[Part of a mature student's application for a place at a residential college for adults.] My main problem . . . has been a conflict between what my background and education seemed to fit me for, combined with a deeply ingrained lack of confidence, and what in my heart of hearts I really wanted to do. I think I can respond imaginatively to the world and to some of the problems of society, but I do need discipline and guidance and feel I could benefit from this and possibly even make a small contribution of my own.

I became dissatisfied with my own efforts at dressmaking. I had picked up what knowledge I had in a totally higgledy-piggledy way and felt I needed some expert help before I wasted any more time and money on making garments I was ashamed to wear. There is no creative satisfaction in making something which turns out badly. I wanted to feel that there was at least one craft that I could do reasonably well.

Sometimes a modest teacher, or one who expects his students to have primarily vocational motives, will be surprised to find that students seem to be stirred and sustained by a genuine wish to extend themselves, as in the early-morning, day-release German class described here by their teacher:

Attendance is always good, and they go to great lengths to inform you if they're away on business. Strangely, few will ever use the language at work or even on holiday, and with most even that will be unlikely for some years, because they have children and usually take their holidays in Devon and Cornwall. Some of the most unsuccessful have persevered, and fought reluctant heads of department who refused permission to have part of the morning off (8.30

to 10 a.m.). I don't know why they do come, right to the end of term. This can be a source of bitterness when most other part-time classes have closed at Whitsun. But they are honestly keen. It could be a means of escape, but I doubt it, because they talk with enthusiasm about their work.

Captive wives

One of the most easily diagnosed and best publicized social problems of the last decade has been the recognition that young mothers and middle-aged wives can feel isolated and trapped by their families and homes. They clearly recognize their own need for self-development, and will certainly provide an increasingly important clientele for adult education, particularly if day-time classes with *crèches* can be made available to them.

These women are usually anxious to improve their general education, either as a preliminary to training for a new career, or simply as a way of proving to themselves and their families that they are still independent individuals capable of intelligent thought. As Hannah Gavron wrote about 'captive wives', 'in a work-orientated society, those who do not work have some reduction in status, and housewives, no matter how arduous housework actually proves to be, do not feel themselves at work.' * Women in this situation will sometimes be happy with any class that makes a reason for getting out of the house, but there seems to be a growing tendency to choose a class which is working towards an examination, since this provides not only a challenging, clear-cut goal, but also one more step towards the world of work and increased self-respect:

Although I hoped to avoid the 'woman's page of the *Guardian*' sort of whiny approach to being a housewife and mother, I nevertheless felt terribly isolated when I was at home all day. All my confidence seemed to evaporate and I felt myself sinking to being my husband's wife instead of a person in my own right. We had an adult education centre literally just round the corner and it has been my salvation really. I always thought it would be rather inferior educationally, but when I read the prospectus I saw they were offering philosophy in the afternoons with someone quite well known taking the class.

*Hannah Gavron, *The Captive Wife*, Routledge & Kegan Paul, 1966; Penguin, 1968.

I felt it would be an opportunity to study something I had always been interested in, to try something difficult and to get me away from the baby for a bit. It has proved difficult all right, but terrifically exciting, a very good way of keeping in touch with what happens outside the home.

Three years ago I began to feel the need to do something outside the home, apart from golf. My family and I do not wish me to go out to work if I can justify my existence without doing so, but I do intend to continue studying, partly because of the satisfaction of being able to study, partly because there is so much to learn and everything I learn helps to make life more interesting, and partly because it's good to feel that after all I am passing my school exams. I have to pass because my children would bust their sides if I failed! I have always found that most things come in useful and if anything should happen to my husband I might be in a better position to help my family.

We may even be reaching the situation where young and middle-aged wives feel guilty if they are not going to some kind of adult education class. Articles now commonly appear in women's magazines round about September, extolling the benefits of adult education and urging women to undertake a class to stimulate their minds. This makes a change from the enthusiastic way in which, in the past, classes have been recommended on problem pages as a way of meeting a husband or making friends.

Social motives

One of the popular myths about adult education is that students only come into it for *social* reasons. Certainly it is not difficult to see that the isolated housewife might have social as well as intellectual motives for coming to a class, or that many other students may have some social hopes of a course; but research shows that the social motive is far from being the most commonly given reason for starting a class in the first place. For instance, only just over 10 per cent of the NIAE's population sample gave it as a main reason.

Nevertheless, it seems clear that for some people it is the prospect of making friends which draws them in. Some students can be quite frank about it, stating their loneliness unequivocally:

I first joined an evening class about six years ago for the simple reason that I felt lonely at the time and needed the social contact.

The subject was only incidental – in this case the history of London. The tutor was dull, spending the whole time either reading from a book or just talking at us. He was not prepared to vary his course to provide a second year – he just did the same year over and over again. Nevertheless I must have obtained something from the class, because I've been interested in the subject ever since.

When my wife died I realized what a very limited life we had been leading. We had obtained all our social and intellectual stimulation from inside our own home. We visited the library regularly, watched television, listened to the radio and we saw just a few close friends and family fairly often. All that changed when she went. My whole way of life became geared to a second education, and I pride myself that I have become an expert on eighteenth-century silver, a fluent speaker of bad Spanish, and an interested spectator of the arts.

Sometimes whole groups of friends and neighbours whose interest appears to be not so much in any particular subject as in the possibility of a night out together will shop around for a class that can take them all. There are students who come because a friend who has joined a class wants at least one familiar face round her. One does hear also of people who turn up on enrolment night and declare quite openly that they want something to occupy Mondays, Tuesdays and Thursdays, so what is available, please. Horticulture, early church music or metalwork – the subject is immaterial. This kind of student presumably must exist since he is discussed so often and so indignantly at adult-education conferences; but in nine years of teaching, enrolling and, latterly, visiting adult classes I have never yet come across him in the flesh, and I suspect that such students form, and have always formed, only a tiny minority of the total adult student body.

It is possible of course that some types of adult education attract the lonely more than others. Edna Smith, Warden of Knuston Hall, a short-term residential college for adults, has noted a tendency for her courses to draw in a large percentage of students whose prime need seemed to be social. One of her applicants wrote:

Would you please book me for courses 26, 27, 28, 29, 30, 32, 34, 35, 37, 38, 41 all on your current list. If you send me the application forms I will fill them in, but I am sending the cheque now to make sure of getting in.

N.B. I notice there is a gap of two days between 26 and 27, and five days between 28 and 29. Please may I stay for these periods! I will gladly pay whatever is due and take part in whatever courses are being held at those times.*

However, such a pathetic cry from the heart is extremely rare, and students who are willing to admit to a much milder version of the same social needs should not necessarily confirm the suspicious adult tutor's worst fears. There is no reason for supposing that students whose prime motive is social will refuse to work. On the contrary, because they need the security of the group and the approval of the teacher, such students are likely to work extremely hard to maintain their prestige. In fact, a group composed of socially inclined students starts at an advantage since the teacher can expect students to get to know one another quickly, and to be more than usually willing to extend the activities of the classroom into walks, excursions, concerts, visits to exhibitions, any or all of which may be effective ways of reinforcing the learning accomplished in the classroom.

Other motives

For a small but steady minority, adult education will offer a last chance for strictly *remedial* education. Others may be attracted by the facilities themselves rather than by the class and the opportunities to learn, so that they may at first resist the teacher's attempts to teach. There is nothing unwholesome about this sort of motive, indeed one of the more promising recent developments in adult education has been the increasing willingness of some principals to offer weekend facilities in sport and the crafts, on the extremely informal basis that a tutor will be available if necessary but that there will be no organized classes. Some of the most promising aspects of this arrangement are that it brings in whole families together, and that it helps to overcome the anxiety problems of adult learners, who undertake strictly what they feel able to cope with in an atmosphere which encourages experiment and growth.

*Edna Smith, 'New courses for "old hands"', *Adult Education*, vol. 40, no. 5, 1968.

Some educationists have attempted to link particular motives with the human life-cycle. They point out that in early adulthood it will be motives linked with finding and planning a home, rearing children, and forging ahead in work which will tend to bring adults to classes. In middle age, developing absorbing leisure interests, coping with teenage children, and coming to terms with frustrated ambition may predominate, whereas in old age the most important motives will be connected with adjusting to retirement and decreasing physical strength, using leisure constructively, and looking for some kind of philosophy of life which can seem to give it meaning. Even so, this kind of classification cannot but seem over-crude in terms of individual students.

Discovering hidden or less obvious motives is much more difficult, but it does seem that of the more devious reasons which bring students to classes, the most important might be the student's wish to test himself. H. A. Jones makes a useful distinction here when he points out that 'the motive to attend may be quite different from the motive to learn, and that what the students are really wanting to learn may be something unconnected with the chosen subject, something about themselves'.* It was evidently this sort of distinction which these teachers had in mind when writing about their students' motives:

My students were the usual range of young middle-aged people, but one motive stuck out a mile – they all wanted to get O-level French because they thought it some magic key to the academic kingdom. If they could do O-level French it would prove something important to them and to their families.

There are twenty students doing the preparatory course in sociology. Of these, I should say a good fifteen are doing it not because they are strictly 'preparing' for the Open University, but because they want to see if they are intellectually capable of this standard of work. Of the others, four have come out of an intense interest in sociology, and one has come because his friend persuaded him to.

In other words, these teachers are saying that it was not the French or sociology as such that interested their students so much as the opportunity to see if they could do something they thought difficult. In the case of the French class, the tutor is also imply-

*H. A. Jones, 'What do they expect?', in J. Rogers (ed.), *Teaching on Equal Terms*, BBC Publications, 1969.

ing that it was the students' idea of what a pass at O-level French meant to the outside world that had attracted them to the class. Similarly, a student may perhaps enrol for Russian because he hopes to impress his friends, or for fencing because it sounds romantically elegant to those who are unaware of how much physical exertion is involved, or for Chinese because it seems both esoteric and difficult.

Reputable or disreputable educationally, perhaps it does not matter very much what a student's motives are at first, since they are so susceptible to change. It can work both ways. A student who comes full of pure and genuine enthusiasm for the subject may quickly lose his intense motivation if the subject is presented dully or if the class is managed badly. Similarly, the student who only comes 'because a friend has come' may turn into an enthusiast in a class where the teaching is lively and the company congenial. In some classes the agreeable social atmosphere is plainly one of the elements which keeps students coming, sometimes perhaps to their surprise. In others, the original mixture of reasons has been totally overlaid by a vividly generated enthusiasm among the whole class for the subject itself. It is up to the teacher to accept and understand the original reason for enrolment and to use this as a way forward to the most dynamic kind of learning he can devise.

Why they leave

When I first started doing adult work, something impelled me to stand in the main entrance herding my people in like a night-club tout. I was very anxious to see if I could keep 100 per cent attendance. If people left, I took it as a personal blow. If someone was away without warning I'd think, watch it, this could be the beginning of the rot.

The classes always started with thirty on the register, but the senior tutor relied on about one-third of them finding it too difficult and dropping out. He told me that this natural wastage saved him the bother of dividing the class.

The freedom of adult students to stop coming to a class is one of the things which makes teaching in adult education a very different proposition from teaching in schools. Sometimes this freedom can be alarming to teachers, leading to the kind of half-joking insecurity described in the first extract above. In other circumstances, as the second extract shows, a high wastage-rate seems cynically encouraged by administrators and teachers alike as a convenient way of coping with large numbers.

Surveys

More usually, the fact that students can and do leave is a source of some watchful concern to everyone in adult education, but it is only recently that any serious and large-scale attempt has been made to find out the main reasons students have for leaving a class. One such survey was made at the City Literary Institute by H. A. Jones, who investigated dropouts amongst its student numbers;* a much larger and more comprehensive survey was part of the NIAE work on adequacy of provision and motivation in adult education (see p. 10). These surveys give useful insights into the pressures operating on students and into the consciously voiced criticisms they feel able to make about classes.

Both the City Literary Institute and NIAE surveys suggest that just over a quarter of all those enrolled will drop out of classes, and that overwhelmingly the main reasons these students give for leaving have nothing to do with the qualities of the teaching. In the City Literary Institute survey nearly three-quarters, and in the NIAE survey over half of those who left said that their absence had been caused either by illness, moving house, changing jobs or by general disturbances in their home lives or at their work. Although this finding might be some comfort to those conscientious tutors who always suspect themselves as the first cause of dwindling numbers, it is still a matter for concern, as, even taken at its face value, it suggests that coming to classes is a marginally important activity for many students and possibly an early casualty of domestic or professional strain.

The second largest category of reasons for leaving a class given to the NIAE interviewers (about one-third of the total) was a collection of dissatisfactions with the class itself, while the third general category – the student's own attitudes – accounted for under a quarter of the total. As in the City Literary Institute survey, those who said they left because of dissatisfaction with

*H. A. Jones and D. R. Glynn, 'Student wastage', *Adult Education*, vol. 1, 1967.

the class were more likely to single out dull presentation than any other feature. The NIAE survey also indicated that nearly one-fifth of all the students who left did so because they lost interest in the subject or became interested in some other subject instead.

More surprisingly perhaps, Professor Jones's smaller survey showed that, of other reasons given by students, there were more people who left because they disliked other students than because they disliked the tutor, an interesting reminder that relationships with other students are important. Each member of the class does not simply exist in his relationship with the tutor, but is affected by the success or failure of the social links established with other members of the group.

As far as the standard of work is concerned, both surveys give some slight ground for believing that rather more of the students who left are likely to feel that the standard of work was too easy rather than too hard. The NIAE survey suggests that they are more likely to criticize a course for being too short than too long, but the class itself for being too long; all of which seems to confirm that adults like to feel stretched and that they enjoy a subject which makes demands on them. What these and other pieces of research do not tell us, of course, is how the surviving students would have felt if things had been changed to suit the dropouts.

These surveys are illuminating, but as with investigations into why students come into adult education at all, it is difficult for even the most sophisticated research techniques to uncover precisely what mixture of motives in precisely what proportions encourage students to give up their class. Students may not know themselves exactly why they left the class, or they may feel ashamed of leaving it – for instance if they found the work too difficult. Because of this they may try to conceal the real reason behind some more emotionally neutral one. How is anyone to judge what is the 'true' reason for leaving a class when a student who has clearly found a course arduous says, 'I'm moving house and the journey will be too trying now.' Is the student disguising from himself the fact that the course was too much for him? Is he saving the tutor's face by offering a pressing 'outside' reason rather than hurt the self-esteem of someone he respects? Is he hiding from the disapproval of the other students because he knows that one more added to declining numbers may put the whole course in jeopardy? Or is it all as simple as it looks?

Any one or more of these reasons may be the 'real' reason. The reason the student gives as his 'main' one for leaving may only be a crystallizing of several other vaguer dissatisfactions. How this works together with the polite concealment practised by many adults can be seen in these accounts of why two students left their classes:

The class was enormous – far too big – and the work not quite what I had been led to believe, but it was the coffee break which finally put me off. The canteen was horribly steamy and crowded. I didn't know a soul, and it seemed to be full of yattering middle-aged women in artists' smocks and beads. I decided to give it up and wrote to them asking for my fee back saying that I'd been asked by my boss to do some extra work. There was some truth in this as one of my colleagues was ill and we were sharing out her work.

I struggled along until Christmas but wasn't really learning much. I decided I must be too stupid to understand Wittgenstein and haven't managed to go back since then. One contributory reason is that I cannot find a suitable babysitter. I suppose I *could* just find someone and if I do and if work eases off a bit I might try to go again. I've paid my fee.

Another proviso about surveys must be that interviewees tend to give the answer they think the interviewer expects. (In both the extracts quoted above, domestic reasons were being used as alibis.) Some revealing answers to the same questions might be produced if surveys were conducted by people quite independent of adult education itself.*

Of course, the dropout rate is by no means an even 25 per cent

* In John and Elizabeth Newson's book about how mothers bring up children, *Patterns of Infant Care in an Urban Community* (Allen & Unwin, 1963; Penguin, 1965) they found significant differences between the sorts of answers mothers gave to the health visitor interviewers, and those they gave to interviewers from the university. For instance, only 63 per cent of the mothers interviewed by the health visitors admitted using 'dummies' for the first year of their child's life, whereas the percentage shot up to 72 per cent when the same question was asked by the more neutral university interviewer.

from every class. There are classes where every member who initially enrolled continues to the end with almost unbroken attendance, just as there are classes where everybody leaves. Common sense and the available research suggest that the classes with faithful members are composed of just the same sort of people as those whose members leave, and that the organization of the course may be more significant than the surveys would suggest at first sight. In the bitterly unpleasant winter of 1962–3 I remember noticing with surprise that in the college where I was working, of three apparently parallel groups (divided alphabetically on enrolment) meeting on the same night, two quickly diminished to minute numbers after January, but in the third a large number of the students went on struggling to the class through snow, ice and fog.

Research on dropouts is still in its infancy. It would be surprising if it was ever possible to plumb to everybody's satisfaction the mixture of domestic circumstances, personal dissatisfactions and teacher–student failures, the tensions which develop in a group and the general class conditions which underlie most reasons for leaving.

The teacher's alternatives

In practical terms, what can a teacher do if he seems to have done everything he ought to have done and still finds himself losing students? A small drop in numbers is to be expected, but even these students may be retrievable. One of the interesting aspects of Professor Jones's survey was that many of those who had stopped coming to classes for at least the last six weeks of the course did not consider themselves to have left at all. This suggests that a brief, friendly, non-reproachful postcard or telephone call to absentees may be a sound practice. Similarly, some tutors make a point of asking people to forewarn them if they know they are likely to be absent. Not only does this show the students that the tutor cares if they fail to appear, it can also make a good deal of difference to preparing work for a class. In the class itself, if the teacher has obviously known in advance about absentees, it makes him seem much less the hapless victim of other people's whims in the eyes of the rest of the class, and therefore more in control of the situation.

If these measures fail and students are still leaving, the danger point is reached when a class with, say, twenty-five names on the register falls below twelve. Minimum membership necessary to keep the class going will vary from one authority to another, but the limit will not usually be below ten. In any case, there is something wrong when a class falls below half its original membership, so that possibly the only measure that will stop the rot is a most rigorous re-examination by teacher and class of objectives and methods. This takes courage, and not every teacher has the nerve to invite, listen to and take account of public criticisms, however tactfully expressed. Failing that, a frank discussion with a more experienced tutor may help diagnose some of the difficulties, especially if he can come and sit in on the class to judge for himself what is going on.

However thinly attended the class becomes, all adult tutors can take comfort from the thought that mere head-counting is only the very crudest measure of success in a class. As many experienced teachers have realized, a student can come to a class for three years and sleep soundly every week after the first twenty minutes.

Who they are

I went to my first class as a teacher in adult education convinced that I would have a roomful of poor old ladies who wanted to do a bit of acting as a way of getting to know other old ladies, with the possibility of fighting over a few old gentlemen at the same time. I thought the coffee break would be the really important part of the evening. Imagine my astonishment when I came into the room and found it full of well-educated, alert, young or youngish people who turned out to be deadly serious about what they tended to call The Craft of the Actor. After one or two classes, one of the few older people there approached me on behalf of the class to ask if I would consider dropping the coffee break as he said they preferred to get on with their work rather than 'waste time' in the canteen. I had to abandon all my plans and rethink the whole course. It was not at all what I had expected.

The striking thing about adults who attend classes or volunteer for industrial training is how unrepresentative they are of the population as a whole. Stereotypes, like the one quoted above, quickly break down when the teacher is faced with a real class.

Reinforcement

For a start, the typical adult student has already had a better than average education. The NIAE survey showed that of the total adult population, about three-quarters left school at fifteen or under and had never had any full- or part-time education since leaving school. In startling contrast, for those who were enrolled as students or said they had been enrolled in the past, the proportions were nearly reversed – only a third of the students had *not* had any education since leaving school. This recent survey only confirms findings from several others, local and national, over many years, which show just as clearly that adult education is a reinforcing rather than a remedial process. Those who have already had a good education want more, while those whose education has been minimal are least likely either to enrol for adult education or to volunteer for industrial training.

One interesting correlation to come out of the NIAE survey was that the better educated younger students tended to be much more critical of the standards of teaching in adult education and were more likely to give poor teaching as a reason for dropping out of a class. Obviously, as well as providing a strong stimulus for enrolling in the first place, better educational opportunities also raise people's expectations and make them more discriminating about the teaching they receive.

Social composition

Since education is so closely linked with social class and occupation, it is not surprising that many surveys also show that professional people are far more heavily represented in classes than they are represented in the adult population as a whole. Even so, highly paid professional people do not predominate in classes. By far the largest single social class represented is the group classified by the Registrar-General as C1 or 'lower middle class' – the young primary-school teacher, the nurse, junior civil servant or clerk, secretary, laboratory assistant or technician. These people are more than twice as prominent in further education classes as they are in the population as a whole. The reverse is true of working-class people, who tend to be under-represented in classes in voluntary adult education. This is not to say that people with the briefest of educational experience and with working-class backgrounds never enrol. Indeed with something near three-quarters of the adult population in this situation it would be extremely surprising if none of them appeared in adult education, particularly in colleges in predominantly working-class areas.

There is nothing particularly puzzling about the strong middle-class hold on adult education. Middle-class people tend to be aware of the advantages of education both for themselves and for their children. Educational establishments do not over-awe them and they are more likely to be familiar with publicity outlets such as libraries. A small change in the style and distribution of publicity and brochures may make an astonishing difference to recruitment. One London borough recently abandoned the staid and conventional printed brochure in favour of a supplement prepared, printed and distributed by the local newspaper. Enrolment increased by 50 per cent and the increase included a significantly high number of working-class people.

These changes may succeed in bringing in some waverers, but perhaps only more radical changes in society as a whole will ever produce a more favourable attitude to that depressingly large proportion of the population – about half – who are revealed by surveys to be resistant to the whole idea of adult education. These non-joiners tend to have a different view from the educationist's of the purpose of classes – a large number were reported by the NIAE survey as thinking that classes were only concerned with training for work. They also tend to have little idea where classes take place, or where they can find out about them.

Age levels

It is the common experience of interviewers conducting surveys into who the students are to discover that many of the people who reject adult education do so because they feel it is something that is only for young people. In looking at figures on age groups from many surveys, including figures obtained from industrial training, it is immediately noticeable that the age group over fifty-five is usually the smallest, even though in the adult population as a whole this age group makes up about a third of the total. Previous education must obviously play some part here, as many more of those over fifty-five will have left school when there were fewer educational opportunities and when the school-leaving age was lower.

It is clear that the lower down the age scale one goes, the more popular adult education is likely to be. The biggest age group of all amongst those joining adult education classes is composed of those who are between eighteen and thirty-four – in the NIAE survey, 44 per cent. Naturally there will be pronounced local differences – for instance, in an area with a predominantly ageing population the proportion of older people will increase. There are differences, too, in institutions. WEA courses, for instance, tend to attract people of rather high average age. The university departments attract more people with higher education than other organizing bodies, but the WEA attracts more people who left school at fifteen than any other adult-education provider.

The predominance of women in adult education is well known. Surveys show that women outnumber men by about three to one, though again, university or WEA classes will tend to be slightly different, attracting rather more men than the proportion drawn to local-authority establishments. Men tend to appear much less often in the 'personal enrichment' kind of class, and much more often in the vocationally based class.

Recent changes

The type of student has always been dictated by the kind of facilities available. Today there are more facilities, which are being offered over a broader front than ever before. For instance, in industry there has been a massive increase in education since 1964, because of the Industrial Training Act, which in effect offers an employer a choice between either taking advantage of a range of inducements to train his employees or, if he refuses to train, paying something towards the cost of those who do. Thus the 1960s saw, for the first time, substantial numbers of people coming into contact with education and training who had had no education at all since leaving school. Similarly, although local-education-authority institutes and further-education colleges have recently suffered some stunting of their growth as a result of government economies, it is still true that they have expanded to a previously unimaginable size.

Even so, all the evidence points to the conclusion that adult education is still very far from being an activity which is likely to involve everyone at some time in their lives. Before this desirable state of affairs can be reached, attitudes to education in the population at large would have to change, and the adult educationist would have to abandon some of his traditional attitudes to recruitment. Instead of expecting people to come to him, he must make approaches to them, not perhaps as individuals but as already existing groups and communities whose needs and interests he can diagnose. It is on this basis that some of the most interesting recent advances in extra-mural education have been made. University departments have approached trade unions, women's organizations or youth clubs, and have arranged courses on a servicing basis. Without this sort of initiative, carried out on a much larger scale than ever before, adult education will undoubtedly grow a little, but in yet glossier middle-class directions – further classes in restoring antiques or understanding the stock market. It might well do this at the expense of the wider mass of potential customers waiting to be drawn in from elsewhere.

Chapter 2
How Adult Students Feel

Anxiety

When I was a very new teacher, I was most unwisely set to do my duty on enrolment night at the college where I was working. One of my first customers wanted to enrol for Beginners' Italian. I asked her, as I had been told to do, whether she knew any Italian and if so how much. She confided cheerfully that this would be her third year in the Italian beginners' class. She particularly liked the tutor, but it was not just that. She still did not feel confident enough of her Italian to progress to the second year. She was afraid of finding it all too much, of looking silly, and that was why she wanted the comfort and familiarity of Beginners' Italian all over again.

This was my first encounter with one of the most striking features of adult students: their anxiety that they might be making themselves look foolish, or that they might be exposing themselves to failure. This sort of anxiety is not confined to the students who come to 'recreational' classes, nor is it confined to the unsophisticated and poorly educated. On the contrary, it seems to apply right across the range of adult students. Out of dozens of pieces of writing I have collected from teachers and students on this theme, I have chosen the illustrations below, not for any particular originality or eccentricity, but because they seem to show the kind of anxieties which worry adult students.

For months before this training course started I used to dream about looking stupid on it, and of making it look that I was incapable of doing the job. I was astonished at myself – a Cambridge first and all – being so worried about going 'back to school', but I used to think to myself, oh well, in another three months, two months, one month, it'll all be over.

We were told we were going to have a 'free discussion' and that we were all going to be expected to speak. That was all right for those who'd been at school more recently than me, but I'd been a mere housewife only a week before and I made up my mind on the spot that wild horses wouldn't drag any 'discussion' out of me. I knew I'd say something silly.

The whole point of drama is that you step out of yourself, and this is what I wanted to achieve, but the self-consciousness which I hoped to lose when I joined the class in the first place was a most severe barrier to shedding it! Every time it came to my turn I'd get butterflies in my stomach, though I tried desperately to conceal my nervousness. Everyone in the class was a colleague of mine and I did not like them to see how afraid I was. Also, never having done any acting before, I knew my performances would be bad and I did not like doing anything badly, particularly in front of people who knew me as an efficient person in other ways.

I've enrolled this year for cookery – but demonstrations only. I don't want to do anything myself. I had enough of that last year – made hundreds of mistakes which was a laugh for everybody else, not much fun for me.

We all know the difficulties of obtaining written essays from students. I believe the reason is that a student who knows he has impressed you in class is afraid you will 'see through' him if he puts anything down on paper. There is often a deep-seated sense of inadequacy in my students, even though many of them are successful professional men and women. They associate written work with tests, marks and examinations, and therefore with potential failure.

You must remember that many of the lads who come here for the shop-steward course left school at fourteen. They are terrified of 'doing writing', so we have to wrap everything up as 'discussion' and establish an atmosphere where they are free to say anything they like without fear of looking daft. The trouble is that I find it almost impossible to find out whether they have learnt anything or not because their self-esteem is so fragile where education is concerned.

Research has even produced physical proof of this sort of fear and anxiety in adult learners. One experiment showed that if blood tests are taken from adults before, during and after engaging in a piece of learning, there is a rise in the level of free fatty acid in the blood as the learning proceeds, a rise which becomes more noticeable and persists longer the older the learner is. Free fatty acid content is a good measure of emotional stress, and a high free fatty acid content can in itself prevent people learning efficiently. Thus the anxiety of the adult who is afraid of looking silly can itself be the cause of a poor performance and can confirm the learner's worst fears. It will be particularly noticeable where a skill like weaving, driving or embroidery is being taught, because fumbling or trembling fingers and the ineptitudes they cause will then be obvious. Experienced tutors in more cerebral subjects will be equally familiar with the blushing, the tense, worried looks and hesitant voices of students who are not altogether confident of their own abilities and judgements.

There are exceptions, of course. Younger students, especially those who have just left school or college, may experience no worries at all because they feel they are in a familiar environment. One young woman, who had graduated in sociology only a few months before, started her description of her experiences in a literature and philosophy class in the following crisp and confident way:

I was really looking forward to joining the class and learning a new subject. I did not feel at all nervous as I have walked into many a lecture hall, and felt fully capable of tackling anything the lecturer was prepared to give me.

This type of student does not expect to find the work difficult and has evidently regarded education as an entirely enjoyable and stimulating experience. Youth and vitality are on her side, and with a degree newly in her pocket she feels she has no cause to be worried by anything in her philosophy class, because it is merely an informal continuation of a process in which she has already proved herself.

There are plenty of other students who will not suffer from feelings of nervousness and tension – for instance, those women who have been going to the same dress-making class, with the same tutor for many years (some classes have been known to continue for sixteen); the people who go to courses where 'teaching' goes on but not necessarily learning (public lectures an hour long followed by five or ten minutes discussion would be an extreme example). Any course where there is no testing of any kind will have relaxed students; but then very frequently in such cases, although there is no anxiety, there is no learning either, because there is no wish for change in either students or teacher.

Obviously, in voluntary adult education at least, anxiety will not be the predominant emotion in students' minds, otherwise they would never enrol at all. Interest and lively curiosity will be much stronger in the majority of students. One must also remember that nervousness can be fairly easily allayed and that although it may indeed be desirable always to keep the atmosphere at least alert, extreme tension in students should not be a major problem after the first few classes. In a well-integrated group the teacher's role in reducing anxiety becomes less central as students realize the work is within their grasp.

Nevertheless, research and common observation show that some tension is always likely to be present when adults are learning, and that this tension is likely to increase and to be more of a handicap the older the student is and the greater the pressure that is put upon him. It is understandable than men and women on industrial-training courses should be concerned about their performance, as very frequently their jobs or promotions depend on how well they do, whether this is re-training for the middle aged or the initial training now given to most new recruits.

Self theory

Quite why students who come to classes voluntarily should feel anxious is more difficult to discover, especially as surveys show that the major clientele for further education is precisely that part of the population which is most 'experienced' educationally and that might be expected therefore to be least frightened of returning to the classroom. Perhaps the worries of many adults about returning to the classroom have a lot to do with the widely held idea that education is a process which only concerns children. Some adult educationists have recently developed hopeful concepts of 'lifelong learning' or 'continuous education', where broadly based education would come to play a major role throughout everyone's life, but this is still very far from being a generally acceptable idea. At present it seems that it is almost as a deliberate denial of his adult status that the mature student submits himself to further education.

Adults are, after all, people who have come to acquire the status of maturity in their own and other people's eyes as husbands, wives, parents, friends, employers or employees. Perhaps this status and self-esteem is less robust than it appears, and is easily threatened when the adult is put back in what may appear to be the subordinate position of the learner.

Some psychologists, searching for a more thoroughgoing theoretical basis for this anxiety, have found it in something called 'Self Theory', and have usefully pointed out what potential conflict is involved when an adult comes to a class (particularly perhaps in academic subjects or any subject where values are involved).* The conflict, according to 'self theorists', is that every adult already has certain well-developed ideas about himself along with his own system of ideas and beliefs. To admit that he needs to learn something new is to admit that these is something wrong with his present system. Many people, although they may dimly perceive their need for new knowledge, may feel so threatened by the challenge to their previous beliefs that they are unable to learn. For instance, a young mother may realize that she needs to learn more about her child's development and may enrol for a class in child psychology. Once there, she may filter out or refuse to understand anything the teacher and the rest of the class say with which she does not agree, as this might be tantamount to admitting that her present way of looking after her child is mistaken and that she has been in some way a 'bad' mother.

This may be why adult students often take refuge in the unconscious subterfuge that what they are learning is really meant for somebody else. I remember a refresher course organized for the whole staff of a college where I was teaching, which everyone was pressed, perhaps clumsily and unwisely, to attend. It was a stimulating and well-planned short course of lectures and discussions conducted by an experienced but retired college of education lecturer. We all attended with much show of grumbling reluctance. Even though most of us clearly enjoyed ourselves at the time and learnt a certain amount, it would have been impossible to find any one of the full-time staff willing to admit that the lectures were aimed at *us*. No, they were meant for 'inexperienced', 'very young' or 'part-time' teachers. To have admitted that we needed instruction would have aimed too sharp a blow at

*C. Rogers, *On Becoming a Person*, Houghton Mifflin, 1961; A. Maslow, *Towards a Psychology of Being*, Van Nostrand, 1962.

our ideas of ourselves as already professionally competent teachers. The unknowable element here is whether we would have learnt more had the course been more tactfully presented to us as an occasion where we could usefully discuss common problems (which it most valuably was) rather than as something which implied we were deficient in some respect (as perhaps we were). As it was there were, every week, one or two people who made a point of shutting their eyes throughout the whole ninety-minute session or who prepared lesson notes and wrote letters, and a few more who conspicuously absented themselves at the last minute with much elaborate apologizing to the lecturer.

The lessons for teachers seem to be that courses must clearly be planned to help adults preserve at least part of their 'self-image'. The value of the students' previous experience must be generously acknowledged, and used as a basis for building up more experience and gaining further knowledge. This will be particularly important on industrial or professional courses, where some element of external compulsion operates.

The adult learner's feelings are going to differ very much from one individual to another and from one situation to another. Mature women students in their first year of a teacher-training course are likely to be more humble and more openly anxious than a group of experienced managers on a short management training course. Adult illiterates, who will frequently travel over city and county boundaries to make sure of finding a class where they will be unrecognized, are likely to be more in need of reassurance and support than a group of adults of all ages and intelligence who come into a local institute for the relaxation and creative enjoyment of the woodwork class once a week.

But whatever the situation, there is likely to be some tension if there is real learning, and since learning takes place best in a calm, unworried and friendly atmosphere, the teacher should take positive action to see that this atmosphere is established right from the start and maintained all the way through the course. Strategies for the first class, a uniquely important occasion in teaching adults, are discusssed fully in chapter 5, but the same basic principles of consciously relaxed friendliness should always be applied.

The teacher's role

Friendliness is important, but it only goes part of the way towards reducing adult anxieties. It is even more important to make sure that students are immediately rewarded when they get something right, to see that everybody is drawn into the discussion, and to devise everybody tasks that they *can* get right. In a discussion, for instance, 'getting something right' can be simply drawing appreciative comments from other students and the teacher – 'Yes, that's an interesting idea', or 'As Mrs Smith said last week', or 'You remember Mr Jones's argument was' – these small and apparently trifling tokens of interest and respect can be important ways of lowering tension and anxiety in adults. At first they must come from the teacher, but it is noticeable that in the most productive and enjoyable adult classes, the role of giving this sort of reward is frequently assumed by other students.

Sometimes more direct ways of reducing individual anxiety will be necessary and good teachers will make constant offers of individual assistance to those who might admit to needing it. Obviously there are limits in time and energy on how much of this intensive help the tutor can actually give. Not all of it can be done in class, otherwise other students suffer. Help that can properly be offered outside the main class-time might be to mark extra work, to have a look at a previously written essay, to stay behind after a class (caretaker willing) to explain a basic principle which a few students do not understand, to prepare individual worksheets for some students to do in their own time, or to lend books and articles. Perhaps the form the help takes does not matter so much as the teacher's obvious willingness to offer it and to undertake it when requested.

Counselling

All this is straightforward enough, because only academic problems are involved. Some people feel that more questionable principles are at stake when it is not academic but personal difficulties which the student brings to the teacher. Clearly a good deal of harm can be done by adult tutors who set up as amateur psychotherapists, but counselling proper is now being seen more and more as an important aspect of teaching adults, because so frequently the academic anxieties and problems of students are inseparable from more personal ones. Teachers who are concerned only with 'recreational' subjects may not be faced so sharply with the personal problems of students, though even in these subjects it is not at all unusual to hear experienced and sympathetic teachers say, 'They bring me all their domestic problems, hoping I can solve them.' In subjects such as literature or drama where values are constantly under discussion, this in itself will encourage students to mention their own experiences. A teacher who gives these experiences a sympathetic hearing may soon find himself involved in counselling, whether he likes it or not.

In full-time adult education, even more clearly, counselling is essential; if formally incorporated into a course it can be an important and valuable way of reducing the feelings of tension and inadequacy which so many adult learners feel, and which are such a barrier to learning. It is, perhaps, one indication of the growing recognition of the importance of counselling that it is incorporated in the work of the Open University (perhaps as a substitute for the 'moral tutor' of orthodox university tradition). Every student sees his counsellor at regular intervals – a necessary and wise method of giving academic and emotional help to students who are obliged to study alone and without the constant support of teachers and other students.

The basic principles of counselling are clear. All counselling must guarantee confidentiality, and the counsellor must be prepared to accept his client totally for what he is. 'Accept' means here 'not criticize', it does not mean 'agree with'. Agreeing, or pretending to agree would put most counsellors in an intolerable situation. The idea behind counselling is that eventually the client must become responsible for himself and deal with his own problems. Many adult students will attempt to force a teacher-counsellor to give practical advice, but most professionals advise that this is a dangerous course, because it may lead the student to depend on the counsellor. They would say that counselling has been successful when the client finds some solution to his difficulties perhaps without realizing the role the counsellor has played, apart from acknowledging that he has been a sympathetic listener.

Counselling is, however, an intricate business. Those wanting further information and detailed case studies will find them in Dr M Cleugh's book *Educating Older People* (Tavistock, 1962) and Alick Holden's *Teachers as Counsellors* (Constable, 1969). A useful brief introduction to counselling adult students can be found in Enid Hutchinson's article 'Counselling – needs to be met' (*Adult Education*, vol. 42, no. 1, May 1969).

Learning and criticism

Sarcasm and ridicule are out of place in any learning situation. They are misplaced in school with children, and are just as unsuitable with adults, who may come to the class in every way the teacher's equal except for the expertise he has in his subject. Adults may also need protection not only from the teacher's ridicule but also from the possibility of hurtful comments from elsewhere. In voluntary adult education there is only rarely any problem of this sort, but in industry there are still occasions where an understandably vulnerable adult will receive instruction in front of workmates who may subject him to intolerable teasing. It should go without saying that all such training should happen in a totally separate place, where a trainee can make his mistakes in peace.

In subjects where discussion forms the core of work, the teacher will be able to find plenty of ways of letting the student preserve his dignity and showing him that he has made a factual error. Where values and not facts are at stake the student's point of view will, of course, be as substantial as the teacher's, and the teacher's job is concerned in this case not with 'correcting' what students say, but only with establishing ways by which they can measure their own opinions against those of the tutor and of other students.

The more difficult moment comes when information is being given and tested, or when the time comes for the adult to practise the skill he is learning. This is the moment when the learner's anxiety will be at its height and the teacher has to exercise most tact and delicacy.

Ideally, the task should be presented so that it becomes virtually impossible for the student to make a mistake, but in practice this is not always possible. For instance, in learning a language the teacher may have prepared drills and tapes for pronunciation practice, but may find that his students still do not realize that their pronunciation needs correction. His interjections must be made as clearly and tactfully as possible and in a way that still allows the student to save face.

This is often a more difficult task than it seems. R. M. Belbin, an industrial-training consultant and an expert deviser of adult-learning situations, comments ruefully on one experience of his while rehearsing a teaching–learning demonstration for a BBC series on teaching adults:

Teaching something complex like chess to mature adults (usually regarded as poor beginners) is an instructive lesson to teachers themselves. Even the sophisticated teacher falls into traps. When practising on a guinea-pig adult just before the live filming on an absolute novice, I was impressed with how easily the middle-aged woman I was instructing was upset and disturbed by the committing of error and by having this pointed out to her. The task set needs to be judged to a nicety. If the task is not right for the level of development of understanding reached we cannot compensate by putting more effort into our teaching. This tends to drive the teacher and pupil alike to frenzy. It is better to switch to a new task and to maintain our theme of continuous achievement.*

Rather than point out a student's mistake, some teachers feel it is better to wait until the student realizes the error himself and then asks for help. This is a good procedure if the mistake will quickly become obvious – for instance, a young housewife in a cookery class who thickens soup by adding egg yolks to the boiling mixture will see straight away that something's wrong because the soup will curdle; a trainee driller in industry may realize immediately that he has made a mistake because the machine will stop. Unfortunately for straightforwardness, not all adult learning can be subjected to 'right/wrong' procedures of this type, and the teacher must find other ways of both allaying anxiety and correcting mistakes.

In an effort to avoid issuing judgements themselves, some teachers try to put the onus of judgement on the learner. For instance, a drama teacher might ask a student to give a speech,

*R. M. Belbin, 'How do they learn?', in J. Rogers (ed.), *Teaching on Equal Terms*, BBC Publications, 1969.

and then ask him to criticize it himself; an art teacher might ask a student to make an appraisal of his own painting. Occasionally this can be done with success, but all too often the technique is to demand brusquely, 'Now what was wrong with that?' A student who was able to overcome his shyness enough to make his speech will usually react by wildly criticizing every single thing he can about his own performance, whether or not he really thinks he is guilty of such faults. Some students are extraordinarily humble, and will often gloomily accept what seems to be the teacher's main premise – that everything is wrong with their work and nothing is right. Self-criticism is an important part of learning, but it cannot be imposed from outside, it comes steadily as skill improves and the characteristics of a 'good' performance are recognized.

It seems better instead for the teacher to try to establish an atmosphere where mutual and constructive criticism is a natural part of the course. This has to be managed with great care. The process must involve the whole group, including the teacher, who should be willing to offer his own work for the same sort of criticism that he demands from everybody else. In other words, he must show that he does not think himself an infallible source of knowledge. Some teachers consider even 'helpful' comments from students on each other's work to be potentially hurtful, and therefore avoid encouraging the situation where it happens. Other teachers, in trying to avoid turning the spotlight of the whole group on to one individual, will ask students to assess one another's work in pairs, but this, too, can bring difficulties, as one teacher shows in the following comment:

I had hoped that I could make the class appreciate my difficulties in assessing their work by asking them to read and criticize, in a constructive sense, their neighbour's work. But I had failed to appreciate their self-consciousness and their great reluctance to show their work to anyone except 'the teacher'. One of the class, a chatty, middle-aged nursery teacher, later told me that several of them nearly decided never to come again after the evening on which I introduced this plan.

Sometimes teachers can be so conscious of the need to alleviate anxiety that they go to the other extreme – their classes are so friendly that no learning is done at all, because the teacher never dares to challenge the students. He has played himself out of his role as teacher until it seems that he has nothing more to offer. Although on the surface these classes seem to be pleasant enough, they often disintegrate in sheer frustration when the students begin to realize that in spite of the pleasant, even self-congratulatory atmosphere, nothing has been accomplished.

At the other end of the spectrum I have heard some teachers, or more particularly some training officers, press the claims of deliberately whipping up anxiety in adult students. 'Keeps them on their toes to be a bit worried, and therefore does them good', is how the argument usually goes. Often this is another way of saying, 'This is how I was taught, and this is how I'm going to teach', implying further that it is only by the effort of the teacher who constantly goads the class into action that any work is done at all. Nobody is claiming that adults should be so relaxed that they go to sleep or don't care, but deliberately to encourage worry is counter-productive. Any teacher who tries it in classes where the students come voluntarily will soon find himself without a class.

Ageing

Anxiety can be overcome, but teachers may find themselves dealing with more subtly destructive forces in the learner's own mind, and this is the adult student's belief that his intellectual powers inevitably suffer serious decay with age. Teachers of languages, for instance, or teachers of any subject where students believe memorizing to be involved, will frequently find themselves being told, and not only by the elderly, 'I can't remember things very easily now – it just won't go in', or 'I'm afraid I'm just not as bright as I used to be'. Even students who say nothing on the topic may secretly be wondering whether their struggles with a subject may not be caused by some inevitable decline of their abilities with age. This is a most important factor for any adult tutor to bear in mind, as particularly in industry many of the students are likely to be over thirty-five.

The phenomenon has been noticed by those researchers who have investigated the effects of ageing on learning. One of the most celebrated of these research projects was conducted by A. T.

Welford at Oxford between 1946 and 1956. In describing results and his methods, Welford comments wryly on the difficulties this belief creates for the researcher:

Most investigators have found difficulty in obtaining middle-aged and old subjects. It is fairly easy to obtain men in their twenties, but in the thirties and over they become increasingly unwilling. Many plead lack of time, or raise other difficulties, or agree to come, then forget. These pleas are, of course, sometimes well justified, but it is quite clear that in most cases they are excuses and that the real reason for unwillingness is fear of being tested and in particular of doing badly and appearing foolish. They seem to know well the popular opinion that as one advances through middle age one's ability falls, and do not wish to have this demonstrated upon themselves.

The fear manifests itself in several ways. For example, typical remarks made by older subjects before being tested are: 'You don't really want me, do you? I shan't be very good.' 'You can't expect too much of me; after all I'm nearly sixty.' 'So this is where you make a fool of me, is it?' After being tested, older subjects almost always ask how they have done and demand to know how their results compare with the average. . . . Visible relief and pleasure are frequently shown by older subjects upon being told they have 'done well'. Yet even when told this many criticize their performances and produce reasons, such as eye-strain, tiredness or preoccupation with other problems, for not having done better. Frequently their actual performances in no way merit this self-criticism.*

Welford was describing an experimental situation where his subjects were being asked to participate in something unfamiliar, where the 'testing' element was likely to be paramount in the subjects' minds because they knew what the researchers were investigating. In such a situation the subjects were likely to be extremely touchy about the relationship between their age and their performance. But this is not so far removed from the classroom situation; indeed the reactions of Welford's subjects may only be unusual in their frankness. Under pressure his subjects may have shown beliefs that many older adult students have, but never quite voice in the classroom.

Whatever the student himself thinks, there is plenty of power-

*A. T. Welford, *Ageing and Human Skill*, Oxford University Press, 1958.

ful popular reinforcement for the idea that, as Shakespeare's Dogberry asserted, 'when the age is in, the wit is out'. Many firms make public their policy of not recruiting anyone over thirty-five, and in spite of the fact that, for instance, airlines will re-train pilots in their fifties to fly new aircraft, it is undoubtedly true that there is a prejudice against the middle aged and elderly at work. Proverbs like 'You can't teach an old dog new tricks' are damaging enough in their way, but perhaps even more harm comes from the words of those academics who have given a certain gloss to the same thought. One of the most famous of these pronouncements came from Sir William Osler in 1905. Osler was a celebrated physician and Professor of Medicine, and when he retired from the Johns Hopkins University at the age of fifty-five to take up a new appointment at Oxford he made a semi-serious speech, jokingly advocating chloroforming those over sixty, and more seriously advising letting the younger men get on with the real business of the world.

The effective, moving, vitalizing work of the world is done between the ages of twenty-five and forty – these fifteen golden years of plenty, the anabolic or constructive period, in which there is always a balance in the mental bank and the credit is still good.

Osler was apparently deeply hurt at the torrent of abusive letters and caustic comments that followed newspaper headlines such as 'Osler Recommends Chloroform at Sixty', but 'Oslerism' had by then entered popular mythology, and for years afterwards people who had never read his speech quoted what they imagined he had said.

More recently, the anthropologist Edmund Leach achieved in his own words a surprising *succès de scandale* not dissimilar to that created more innocently by Osler over sixty years before. In the Reith Lectures for 1967 Leach spoke coolly but provocatively of the way galloping technological change was creating entirely new kinds of knowledge, and how it was making the opinions and skills of the elderly irrelevant to present-day and future life:

In our runaway world, no one much over the age of forty-five is really fit to teach anyone anything. And that includes me. I am fifty-seven. It is hard to accept but that's just the point. . . .

Medical science is steadily increasing the expectation of life and this, combined with the concentration of industry into larger and larger units, is having the effect that an ever greater proportion of the final power of decision is being concentrated into the hands of very old men, which is the worst possible way of facing the problems of a rapidly changing future. Since those who hold offices of power will never willingly give them up, I believe that there is only one solution to this problem. The young must somehow or other enforce quite arbitrary rules of early retirement. In those parts of our systems which are concerned with research and technological development, either in education, or in industry, or in politics, no one should be allowed to hold any kind of responsible administrative office once he has passed the age of fifty-five.*

The total effect of the adult student's own and other people's belief in his declining ability to learn with age may create quite severe difficulties for the teacher of adults, particularly in a class where older people predominate. Students may use their age as a crutch to avoid the discomfort of real learning, their whole attitude may imply 'You mustn't work me hard, because I'm old.' They may unconsciously be working at very much less than full pressure because they are afraid that if they really try they may really fail; they have lost confidence in their ability to work at full intellectual capacity.

The teacher faced with this situation has somehow to encourage the student to believe that although there is some decrease in intellectual capacity with age, this is negligible compared with more important factors such as native intelligence, education or even practice. Some teachers will say this bluntly to students, but they run the risk of having a student say, 'But I never got much education and I was never very bright in the first place, so what hope is there for me now?' Brightly encouraging remarks from a tutor may have their place, but there is nothing to equal the encouragement a student feels when he can see for himself that he is making progress. Designing a situation where this can happen will be one of the tutor's strongest weapons against anxiety in older students.

Even so, it is bound to be true for many adults that they feel some loss of confidence as their physical appearance changes

*Edmund Leach, *A Runaway World?*, BBC Publications, 1968.

with age; they may feel depressed about the loss of responsibility as their children grow up, or anxious about whether automation is likely to do them out of a job. They may be bitter or disillusioned as ambitions remain unfulfilled, a situation not improved by our current obsession with youth and youthful achievement. This is a gloomy picture, an exaggerated one perhaps, but research studies tend to support the idea of 'crisis' with ageing. Indeed some people suggest that we ought to be much less concerned with the stresses and problems of the adolescent and much more concerned with those of the middle aged and elderly.

Social background

The adult learner's attitude towards himself is also deeply affected by social class. One of the most revealing themes in Margaret Powell's frank and funny autobiographical books* – unique and unpretentious pieces of sociological material – is how absolute and unchangeable the social structure seemed to a domestic servant. The privileges of education, like the privileges of comfort, were accepted as being the natural prerogative of the rich. It has taken Margaret Powell, a sturdy and tireless spirit, most of a lifetime to reach the stage where she could aspire even to O-level English, and her account in *Climbing the Stairs* of her brushes with adult education ought to be read by every teacher. Many who were less confident, less persistent have never even come that far.

Working-class attitudes

Statistics have shown again and again how, even in the 1960s, thousands of able working-class children dropped out of full-time education. For instance, the percentage of working-class children now going to university is much the same as it was before 1939. The reasons are obviously complicated, but if a home has few books, if parents see the school as remote and even hostile, if simple information about education is lacking (for example, that grants are available for university students) then it is likely that children in such a home will drop out of education early and go into jobs much less demanding than their abilities would warrant. Not all working-class children have the constant

Below Stairs and *Climbing the Stairs*, Peter Davies, 1968, 1969.

prodding and support from their parents that many middle-class children have, and financial considerations may press hard. The practice of streaming by ability in schools quickly becomes a self-fulfilling prophecy, and individual children's records show how once a child is graded C stream, he conforms to what a teacher expects of a C-stream child. By the time this child has become an adult he sees himself as a C-stream person, incapable of making an A-stream response.

It is difficult to generalize here and exceptions are legion, but several studies show not only the detailed mechanisms of such processes but also how personality patterns established in child-hood and contributed to by education and social class together tend to encourage an attitude where many working-class people think that education is not for them. They tend to believe that they are meant to be followers rather than leaders, expecting to be dominated and controlled, often resentfully, but still playing the subordinate role. The C-stream child may grow up to be an adult who can only find a menial job, and many people have pointed out how working-class people whose education and jobs have accustomed them to being ordered and controlled by other people may find it difficult as adults in education to assume responsibility themselves. On the other hand, middle-class people will tend not to be afraid of headmasters, to know their way round education, and indeed will even describe the advantages of something like public-school education in terms of having been an 'education for leadership'.

This is a caricatured view of a complex social-class structure, but social class is one important part of the adult learner's back-ground and it will affect the way he approaches learning. In many cases it will determine whether he undertakes further education at all, since social class is a major factor in distinguishing those who are participants in adult education and those who are not. Given that adult education appeals strongly to the middle class and to those who already have a good education, it should not surprise anyone that class will affect the student in the learning situation itself, influencing the amount of responsibility the student feels he can undertake for his own learning and the way he reacts to the teacher and to other students.

Memories of school

Whatever his social class, every adult student comes to further education with a well-developed set of expectations about what it will be like. Inevitably these expectations are governed very largely by the student's experience of education as a child, and these experiences will considerably influence the way the teacher is able to conduct the class.

In industry there may, for instance, be severe problems with adults who are working on semi-skilled jobs and have to be re-trained to keep a job at all. Many of these people may be the grown-up products of the type of education whose desperate shortcomings John Partridge described so well in his closely observed account of one year in the life of a secondary modern school.* His comments on the low level of motivation towards learning in the school can stand as a reminder to the adult tutor or training officer of attitudes that may be even more deeply entrenched in maturity:

Firstly, English education, as seen by these boys, consists of preparing for examinations and little else; but these are the boys who have failed every test and examination they have ever taken, so that asking these boys to take their work seriously is like suggesting to prisoners of war that they should voluntarily undertake eight hours daily combat training. Since we spend so much time and energy on grading and examining children, we can hardly expect those who have constantly failed to be exceptionally keen for the next round.

This type of child is all too happy to be waved off the school premises at the minimum legal age. As an adult he may have a deep suspicion of 'education', and is certainly unlikely to enrol voluntarily for 'night school', even if it might be of direct vocational advantage if he did so.

In industry, where for various reasons he may be obliged to undertake further education, tremendous allowances must be made for his likely attitudes. For instance, no one will use the word 'education' because that sounds too much like studying a subject for its own sake. Instead it will be called 'training', which

* John Partridge, *Life in a Secondary Modern School*, Gollancz, 1966; Penguin, 1968.

is not so alarming, and many 'training officers' will be anxious to stress their affinities with the chap on the shop floor. They will go to great pains to avoid resembling either the tweedy, seedy, patched-elbowed teacher-figure of tradition, or the 'overdressed arrogant men who use long words to embarrass and trap people' which one child described in a competition on 'The school that I'd like'.*

Instead, many training officers go to almost comic lengths to create a kind of Andy Capp atmosphere where social distance is instantly reduced and where the idea is that if attitudes to the teacher can be changed, that is at least one barrier out of the way. Oddly enough this type of adult student may not be at all resistant to 'new' methods and the training officer is playing one of his strongest cards when he is able to say that the methods *are* new, that they *do* work, that they will be totally unlike anything the adult experienced at school. This kind of announcement can bring nothing but relief to adults who loathed and detested almost every moment at school, and whose dread of industrial training can largely be reduced to a fear of it turning out to be just like school.

Student expectations

Those who were a little luckier in their parents' social status, or more fortunate in their previous educational existences, may bring with them equally firm ideas of what they expect from a teacher and his methods. Firstly, in spite of wanting due deference paid to the fact that they are adults, many adult students may still feel a teacher ought to be a rather remote, god-like figure. They may consider it rather improper for a teacher to be too friendly. Confusion and embarrassment sometimes result from a teacher's first attempts to establish a relaxed atmosphere – for these students it is too much like seeing 'Sir' pick his nose or engage in any other ordinary human activity. Fortunately this sort of shyness is easily broken down, especially in a group which contains plenty of students who have attended other adult-education courses, and who can show newcomers how to put a teacher in his place.

Secondly, and in practice inextricably mixed with attitudes to

* Edward Blishen (ed.), *The School that I'd Like*, Penguin, 1969.

the teacher's role, students may have firm expectations about teaching method, based again on their experience at school or in higher education. Even those who had only modest success academically are still likely to feel that the methods they already know are best because they are the only ones already familiar.

A student who has been out of touch with education for a long time, or who is under a misapprehension about 'modern' methods, may fiercely resist a teacher's attempts to introduce a different kind of education, even though, paradoxically, the 'new' methods may be clearly both more enjoyable and in the long run more effective. This particularly applies to subjects with which adults have already had some acquaintance. Although many adult students will come to classes in, say, English because previous methods have failed, they will still expect the conventional methods with grammar to be employed, because they blame themselves for previous failure, not the teaching method. They frequently think that if only the *same* method could be employed but more intensively, then all their problems would be solved. They may also feel, as a result no doubt of the irrelevance of much of their previous education, that learning and their own lives have nothing in common, that 'real' education is something remote and separate. The tutor's attempts to solicit and 'use' the student's own experience of life may for this reason meet with incomprehension. One English teacher describes here the practical difficulties these sorts of problems created in a course in English:

Most of the class, but especially the overseas students, felt that I ought to be teaching them in the formal notes-on-the-blackboard, do-this-and-you-will-be-successful style they remembered from their own schooldays. They found it difficult to grasp the fact that copying into notebooks pious dicta on what constitutes an essay is no substitute for trying to write one. Only slowly have they come to realize that they have each amassed a store of experiences which, though apparently trivial, could supply them with essay material for the year. For the first month I read their essays with despair; the prospect of finding a mark scheme to cover such a wide range seemed impossible. Yet this, too, they seemed to regard as essential, and I soon discovered that all my tactfully worded suggestions for improving style and content, punctuation and spelling, were regarded as mere stalling on my part, a refusal to get down to the real business of the course. Eventually the hard core of enthusiasts who survived after Christmas accepted my methods. I, too, had learned to compromise and in some measure give the sort of instruction they expected in return for a show of participation from them.

Other versions of the same basic situation may be found throughout the whole range of adult education: students who come to learn languages and are disconcerted *not* to be given lists of irregular verbs to memorize; trainees in industry who expect to be *told* how to understand a chemical process and are surprised to find themselves faced with programmed instruction instead; people who come to art classes thinking that the first thing the teacher will do is to expound on the laws of perspective and are astonished to find instead that they are painting pictures straight away; literature students who may think that there is a 'correct' view of a novel or play and that somehow the teacher will convey this to them without any real thought being necessary or proper on their part.

Wherever adult education happens there may be a discrepancy between what the students expect and what the teacher proposes to do. The older the students are, the more their previous learning experience was likely to have been 'passive', since they were at school when the emphasis was on teaching rather than learning, and education was regarded as something that was done *to* you, and not something to which you made a major contribution yourself.

Frequently a change of method will be welcomed with delight by adult students, but sometimes the adult's longing for the 'old' methods has deep roots, not just in his previous education but in his motive for joining. He may sit patiently enough through several weeks of 'modern' method, still waiting for the teacher to reveal the magic key which will effortlessly unlock every secret of the subject, and because of this he has paid no attention at all to what has been happening in the class. He has brushed it aside as padding – 'a refusal to get down to the real business of the course'.

Similarly, attempts by craft teachers to broaden the subject by introducing discussion on materials or standards may meet with polite tolerance, while students wait for a teacher to get back to what they think is the more important task of teaching them how to cut out a dress or de-coke an engine. In craft classes students may expect individual attention and may be puzzled or hurt at the teacher's attempts to introduce methods where group teaching and learning is established. Even in the sophisticated WEA or extra-mural class the students may expect the teacher to dominate and control a discussion to a greater extent than he may feel right. The students may interpret this behaviour as intellectual feebleness or even laziness.

This is why it is essential to discuss right at the beginning not only the course and syllabus but also the method of teaching, so that students know what to expect (this point is developed in chapter 5). It would be very rare indeed to find an adult class stubbornly unwilling even to try an unfamiliar method, but the method itself, like the course, should be constantly under review by teacher and students and the appropriate modifications made by both parties:

I was teaching French to children in a grammar school during the day, using what I considered to be a very good audio-visual method. I saw no reason why my adult class should not learn the same way and they very nobly agreed to try.

I met my first snag in the first five minutes – no books. No books? They *demand* books, nicely, of course. I say they cannot have books until at least the sixth week when they will be familiar with certain sounds and patterns. Rebellion subsides. Second snag – five minutes later – several of them sneakily trying to write things down according to some dreadful phonetic script of their own. I explain about listening and speaking, *they* explain they must see things written down, otherwise they can't remember. We have this very polite battle lasting three weeks. They begin to see the advantages of the language lab and slide projector and the constant repetition – variation – drilling, I begin to see that they really do need the reassurance of the book. On the fourth week I give out books, they sigh with relief as at the appearance of old friends, pronunciation slips a bit, but general progress seems to be faster. It's not Direct Method, but it seems to suit my class.

Chapter 3
How Adults Learn

It has in fact been established that if we were to reverse the natural order of things and keep children away from school while sending their parents there instead, we could teach the parents the same thing for about a quarter of the expenditure in time and money.
JOHN MCLEISH

The previous chapter was concerned with the interior stresses and strains felt by adult learners. This chapter is about what is known from experience and from experiment about how adults learn, how ageing affects learning, and what the practical implications are for the teacher of adults.

What is learning?
Unfortunately there is hardly any subject among psychologists which arouses so much disagreement as learning. There is no one theory which can satisfactorily explain exactly how learning takes place, and which can give guidance to a teacher on how to help adults learn effectively and enjoyably. Although the study of learning has now been under way for nearly a century, it is still probably in its pre-Copernican stage; no doubt in the future the information we now possess will look laughably primitive.

The great bulk of learning research has been into the behaviour of animals. What little human behaviour has been studied has necessarily been restricted to innumerable small-scale laboratory experiments, and to 'field studies' in classrooms where even a sensitive investigator finds it difficult to define the essence of relationships. Recent industrial studies have added to our knowledge of how some simple skills can be most effectively learnt, but it is difficult and probably dangerous to generalize about how these studies can be applied to the intricacy of individual classroom situations. The suggestions made in this chapter about learning are therefore intended as pointers only, not inviolable laws.

The problem of defining what learning is has itself been the source of much controversy, since no one is really sure whether learning a 'sensori-motor' skill (any skill concerned with the coordination of senses with muscles) and learning to solve an intellectual problem are all part of the same general process. Most psychologists seem agreed that the one basic requirement is that some *change* must take place in the learner. One distinguished psychologist, Kurt Lewin, has suggested that there are four different kinds of learning: a change in cognitive structure (for instance, acquiring and understanding new knowledge, such as learning history or philosophy), a change in motivation (for instance, learning to like or dislike something), a change in ideology or fundamental belief (for instance, changing one's views on communism or race prejudice), and achieving control of the body musculature as one does in learning a skill.*

Just as the basic principles of good teaching apply as much to adults as to children, so it looks as if the basis of learning is the same in children and adults: strong motivation and plenty of activity. The differences are ones of emphasis rather than fundamental principle.

In spite of the often depressing results of research into learning and ageing, the general conclusion reached again and again is that adults *can* learn efficiently. If the way they are invited to learn is geared to their own particular needs and interests they often not only do as well as younger people, but can even outstrip them. Although ageing does have effects on intellectual and manual performance, this will vary very much between one person and another. If any general rule can be made it is that the older people are, the greater individual differences between them are likely to be governed not so much by ageing as by basic intelligence, occupational level and education. Differences within age groups grow more pronounced with age. Highly intelligent sixty-five-year-olds are more likely to have retained their intelligence than those of the same age with poor intelligence, who are likely to have slipped even further down the scale.

With these general provisos in mind, these seem to be the main features of adult learning: adults seem to learn best when they do not have to rely on memorizing, but can learn through activity at their own pace with material that seems relevant to their daily lives and uses their own experience. Finding 'right' answers at the first attempt seems important. Generous practice will rein-

* Kurt Lewin, *Resolving Social Conflicts*, Harper & Row, 1948.

force new skills. Adults who have been out of touch with learning can often improve their educational performance dramatically if they are helped by 'learning to learn'.

Learning by activity

Short-term memory

One of the most important results of research into ageing has been to pinpoint the significance of 'short-term memory'. This faculty is easily disturbed as ageing advances. What seems to happen is that information is received by the brain, which scans it for 'meaning' in order to 'decode' it at some future date. It looks as if the actual capacity of the short-term memory itself may not change too much with age – a young man and a man in his late fifties would both be able to remember and repeat an average of eight random numbers recited to them. But what does change is that if the older man is asked to remember something *else* between the time he is first given the numbers to memorize and the time he is asked to repeat them, he will be much less likely to remember the original numbers than the young man. This is because the 'scanning' stage is more easily disrupted by other activities in older people.

In everyday living one experiences this as a minor nuisance – a telephone number forgotten while one looks up the STD code, the first part of complicated direction-finding instruction confused with the last because the last 'first lefts' and 'second rights' have interfered with remembering the first. In more formal learning, however, the decay of short-term memory (which might already have become noticeable by the late twenties) is more than just a mild social embarrassment or a personal irritation. It can be a serious bar to further progress, or indeed to any progress at all if learning something new and complicated is thought of as presenting a series of pieces of short-term memorizing, any one of which might 'interfere' with its predecessor. For instance, threading up some sewing machines consists of at least six stages, and a beginner could still be trying to remember whether checking tension comes before or after threading the needle, while the teacher is confusing her by demonstrating how to pin out a paper pattern.

Students may not realize that their understanding of some process is defective because of confusion in short-term memory. Many adults are often convinced that they have understood something perfectly when they have failed to understand it at all. Others will realize their confusion and, unless they are particularly bold spirits, will be too timid or too polite or too respectful of the teacher's prestige to ask the question which might solve the difficulty. Instead they remain anxious and muddled, not the best state of mind for learning.

The implications of the decay of short-term memory are that in the classroom a teacher should try to cut down to an absolute minimum the amount of conscious memorizing that has to be done by the student. 'Memorizing' means not only looking at a list and trying to learn it, but also includes activities such as listening to lectures, following verbal instructions given all at once, and watching demonstrations which the student has to copy later. The demands of the subject and the time and money available for planning resources will dictate how memorizing can be cut down, but, for instance, instead of expecting the dress-making novice to remember from verbal instructions or demonstration how to thread up a sewing machine, the teacher could direct a student to follow a large and clearly labelled diagram. Better still, she could prepare a specially labelled and numbered machine for students until threading up became rapid and sure. With subjects such as history, where a different kind of memorizing may be involved, charts or maps could be used for reference, while attention is concentrated on more important matters. Even in language teaching, most often associated with rote-learning and heavy reliance on memorizing, a language laboratory can help circumvent the need to memorize as whole patterns are built up naturally through constant practice.

The pace of learning

Closely allied with the decline in short-term memory is the effect of age on the pace at which adults can learn and work. In industry, people over forty-five frequently change from conveyor-belt work to something where speed is not the all-important factor, because they are aware of their own slowing up. Older people are often inclined to sacrifice speed for accuracy and prefer to take much longer making sure that they have something just right. Certainly it has been observed both in real industrial situations and in experiments that one of the causes of this slackening in pace is that the older people are, the more extra information they like to have before making a response. For example, in experiments where something not unlike shove ha'penny was tried with adults of all ages, the young people made their moves swiftly and without much thought, whereas the older people carefully measured up distances and hesitated for some time before venturing a throw. Scores of different experimenters have shown that if the adult is asked to learn something new *under time pressure*, the older he is, the more likely he is to become confused and make mistakes. On the other hand, and hopefully, if a man of say forty-five is matched in a task with one twenty years his junior with no clock-watching involved there will be little or no difference in their performances.

Clearly, then, it is essential for adult students to be allowed to work at their own pace. In industry, training schools have found, literally to their cost, that set training periods of perhaps three weeks with formal examinations at the end produce a high failure rate, even though the trainees have frequently been offered (and have refused) an extra training period. Changing to a system where there is no set length for training, where assessment and not examination is employed, and where trainees come in at different times and not in batches together usually produces a consistently better success rate.

It follows that competition with one another and exhortations to 'keep up with the others' are not appropriate for adult students because competition is only another way of introducing pacing. It is better for an adult to measure his progress against his own previous performance rather than to attempt frantic rivalry with his neighbours. This is easier said than done when so much of education is conducted on competitive lines (mark-lists with individual placings, prizes for best work and so on) and when so much stress is put on speed and competition in work and social life. Michael Barratt Brown has described the kind of outstanding contribution that can be made by so-called 'slow learners' when a totally uncompetitive and protective environment was established on their day-release courses.

. . . it needs to be said that tutors of trade-union classes soon learn that our society puts an enormous premium upon mental speed – quickness of grasp and response. This is part of the whole competitive environment in which we are brought up – in the home, at school, in the eleven-plus, in the labour market and at work. The quick thinker wins and the slow thinker is lost and may never catch up. Yet it is our experience that, given time and an uncompetitive environment, the greatest advances, the most profound contributions, the real intellectual exercising comes as much from the slow ones as from the quick ones. Again and again, when philosophical questions are raised it is not the quick ones with the grammar-school and technical education but the slow plodders, grappling with new ideas until they master them, who get to the heart of the matter.*

When no allowance is made for the increase in individual differences which age and experience bring, when the decline in short-term memory is ignored, and where the teacher simply plunges on bearing the whole load of information-giving himself, packing every moment with fresh and complex detail, then some classroom situations of monstrous futility and waste can develop, as described here by a supervisor on day release from industry :

I have never in my life found such terrible teaching as on the term's course of lectures we had on industrial law. For a start I couldn't see why supervisors had to do law anyway, but in any case we didn't learn any. I used to jot down a few notes, it was less boring than doing the *Mirror* crossword like some people did – I used to swear that the lecturer would never have noticed if the whole class had played noughts and crosses because once he'd started it would have taken an earthquake to stop him. His method was to introduce the week's topic, define it so quickly that the definition could have flown out of the window before you could take it in, say 'Any questions?' and then without waiting for the answer plod on to the rest in his usual loud deadpan voice for an hour and a half non-stop. It was completely remote from our actual work and if you did try to understand there were so many legal terms that you could never remember one from another. At the end of the lesson he gave us printed notes on what he'd been talking about – he was a conscientious chap really – but these only made it worse because they weren't at all the same

* Michael Barratt Brown, *Adult Education for Industrial Workers*, NIAE, 1969.

as what he'd said in the lesson. His method of finding out if we'd understood was to suddenly spring a 'test' on us. Presumably he found out how we were doing but we never did, we never saw the papers again and he never gave us the marks, though we did ask. I'd been on a residential course where I'd learnt more in a few days than in a term at this place, so I knew it was all rubbish. I complained to the senior lecturer but it didn't do any good, the next day-release course had him, just the same.

Use of the lecture technique

From this description it would be hard to imagine a style of teaching less suited to adult needs – no class participation, a strenuous pace adopted throughout at which everyone was obliged to 'work', heavy reliance on verbal memorizing, no idea given to students of how they were progressing (no 'knowledge of results'), and a confusing 'reinforcement' (printed notes). Yet this teacher, who the student reluctantly admits was 'a conscientious chap really', obviously took his job seriously. No one who talks continuously for one and a half hours in a classroom and also prepares copious notes for students could be described as totally neglectful, only unaware of the inadequacy of his no doubt painstaking efforts.

In adult education, and indeed to a lesser extent, in industrial training, innumerable classes exist where the teacher does most of the talking, whether this is by lecturing or by demonstrating. Walter James has pointed out how strong the 'lecture-sermon' tradition of the nineteenth century still is, with its 'from the pulpit style', and quotes a report made in 1960 by a WEA working party which commented sadly that a tutor who talks 75 per cent of the time 'is not a rarity'.* Some tutors who enjoy talking, and know they are good at it, will say defensively that their classes often compliment them on their lovely performances and that their personal charisma is what draws students in. This may be so, but whether it *keeps* students, and whether, furthermore, it keeps out more than it keeps in, and whether students are actually learning, is another matter. One study made by John McLeish emphasized how little students retain of information

*Walter James, 'Group dynamics theories', *Adult Education*, vol. 37, no. 3, 1964.

in lectures – less than half was recalled immediately and after a week it had dropped to between 15 and 20 per cent of the total.*

There is a place for a well-planned, well-delivered lecture in teaching adults, particularly where an emotional stimulus is needed or where information can and should be given quickly and conveniently to a group whose individual members are all at the same stage of development. The ability to give a witty and eloquent lecture can be an invaluable and legitimate part of a teacher's armoury of skills. Notes or check-lists might be provided here to reinforce information given. Even so, uninterrupted lectures are only rarely suitable.

Even eloquence can be an untrustworthy tool. Many lecturers become so carried away that they leave their audiences way behind:

One lecturer used to glow with excitement as he spoke. His enthusiasm was terrific and he was a most articulate speaker. He never paused at all, but he often used to say at the end 'Well, that's the first time I've ever felt I've understood that topic.' It never occurred to him to ask whether *we* had understood it! Usually we were lost after the first five minutes though everyone used to enjoy his performance.

The 'broken lecture' with frequent pauses for genuine discussion is probably less tedious for the listeners, more likely to allow for individual differences, and also more likely to show whether or not the lecture is being understood. Far too many lecturers and demonstrators assume that their listeners have some hole in the head into which information can conveniently be poured. As Carlyle said, 'too much faith is commonly placed in oral lessons and lectures, to be poured into like a bucket is not exhilarating to any soul'.

In general it would seem that 'activity' learning is much more suitable, because once they have tried it most adults greatly prefer it to the passive, polite, imitative stuff which they have previously encountered. 'Activity' here means learning through the individual's own decision, experience and participation. Group discussion, therefore, would be more appropriate than listening to one person talk, individual practice more appropriate than just

* John McLeish, 'Student retention of lecture material', *Cambridge Institute of Education Bulletin*, vol. 3, no. 3, 1966.

watching a demonstration. The best way round the suspicions of a group to whom such methods are unfamiliar is to let students try them, without fuss and straight away. If the methods work and if students can see they work, the problem will fade away. If progress is slow or dubious, techniques can be modified after discussion.

Written instructions

In an attempt to design methods of learning by which adult classes can learn at their own pace, some teachers provide students with individual sets of written instructions which students work through at a speed they set themselves. For instance, one second-year car-maintenance class uses printed, plastic-covered sets of drawings plus step-by-step instructions for servicing a dynamo or checking and adjusting brakes. The students in this class work in pairs, and it would be unusual to find any two pairs wanting to work at once on the same part of the old Morris Minor chassis and engine used for class work. The teacher in this class makes occasional use of group demonstrations when some general point seems to be cropping up. More usually he does not appear to be teaching at all. He behaves like a 'resource consultant' available for advice when needed rather than someone who imposes a single pace on the whole class.

Written instructions certainly work with this class, but experiments show that they are more likely to be useful when a learner is already fairly competent (the car-maintenance class were not beginners) and only needs a quick check-list or mnemonic for reassurance. Written instructions must also be designed with care. Several experiments, such as those by Sheila Jones, show that short simple sentences using active tenses are better than long complex ones using the passive tense. People also seem to understand positive statements more readily than negative ones containing the words 'not', 'except', 'unless' or 'otherwise'. If a teacher of photography was composing written instructions for absolute beginners on how to load a 35-mm camera, it would be dubious practice for him to write as follows, even with an accompanying drawing:

* Sheila Jones, 'The design of instruction', *Training Information Papers*, no. 1, Department of Employment and Productivity, 1968.

Care should be taken when removing the cassette from its packaging not to expose it to the light, as this may damage the film. The back of the camera should be opened exposing the spool. The protruding tag of film should be pulled out until about four inches is exposed, shiny grey side downwards, after which the cassette can be clipped into the space on the right and the film drawn across the back of the camera until the end can be fitted into the slot of the spool and fitted on to the sprocket. If the film is not firmly in place it may be scratched or stick when wound on.

This difficult instruction could be improved by writing it in a simpler, more positive way:

1. Draw the curtains of your room to protect the film from too much light as you take it out of the box.
2. Open the back of the camera. You will see a spool on the left, a space for the cassette on the right.
3. Pull out about four inches of film. The shiny grey side is the sensitive side. Keep this face down and clip the cassette into place.
4. You can now draw the film across the back of the camera. Fit the loose end of film into the slot on the spool and see that the sprocket is gripping the sprocket-hole firmly.
5. Check that the film is firmly in place. This will prevent loose ends scratching or sticking.
6. Wind the film on about one inch and close the camera.

Written instructions will obviously be most useful to a well-educated group, since it is accepted that poorly educated students usually find it difficult to cope with 'writing'.

Learning through realistic and relevant material

Adult students like to feel that what they are learning is going to be useful and relevant in their daily lives. They also learn more rapidly the closer resemblance between the learning task and the skill they finally hope to attain.

Problems of 'translation'

It seems that one of the features of adult learners is their difficulty in coping with what are called 'translation' processes. This means that adults find learning a mental or manual skill more difficult if they have to 'translate' instructions or processes from one medium to another. For instance, someone learning to use a lathe really needs to learn the skill by actually using his hands and body. The more processes that are interposed (like reading, writing or watching a demonstration) the longer he will take to learn. Similarly, a student learning to weigh the value of one kind of historical evidence against another needs to plunge straight away into historical documents rather than hear or read someone else's opinons about them. A student learning to speak a language should learn it by speaking himself – reading and writing will only slow his progress.

In industry, training schools are careful to make the training exercises as like the real thing as possible, otherwise the trainee may come to rely so much on the oversimplified task he has learned in the training department that this learning positively interferes with the competent performance of the real-life activity. Similarly, in adult education, a student who has been going to classes in Spanish and has had a tutor who has much too help-fully simplified and slowed down Spanish pronunciation for him may find that in Spain he cannot understand anything very much or extend his own Spanish. He has relied too much on the special 'cues' given him by the tutor. In some kinds of management training, artificial analyses of situations may seem hopelessly over-crude when the trainee is back in the complexity of the real world.

The real thing

Adults are also less tolerant than children of learning 'for its own sake', or of ways and means of learning which seem to be a substitute for the real thing. For instance, one teacher has re-counted that patients of subnormal intelligence in a mental hos-pital were upset when they were given cardboard coins in classes and that real coins quickly had to be substituted. One of the classical studies of adult learning was made by E. L. Thorndike in the early years of the twentieth century. He discovered that where the learning he asked his subjects to perform was regarded as 'useful' to their work, older subjects sometimes did even better than youngsters; where they regarded the learning as 'artificial' they did very much worse.

The lessons here seem to be that in industry the techniques

taught on the training scheme must be as like the final skill as possible, and that in all adult classrooms the materials used, the problems exposed and the methods engaged should be recognizable to the student as relevant and useful to his daily life. When methods such as role-playing or projects are used they should be seen to have real point, otherwise they can begin to look like meaningless, childish exercises, as in this local-history class, where a seasoned and tolerant student comments on the project plans of a new tutor:

We had this very nervous young school teacher taking us and he had ideas about using his school methods with adults. You could see some of the old biddies mumbling when he told them to buy three books – all expensive – and when he followed this up by saying we'd all compile scrapbooks they all went quite indignant on him. Actually I don't want to compile a scrapbook either. What's the point? It's just a game and we'd all be going to a lot of trouble for nothing. He must have guessed we weren't enthusiastic because that was the last we heard of the scrapbook idea.

Using experience

Along with the general slowing down in pace, it may be true that mental processes are likely to become more rigid with age. Some experiments have shown that on problem-solving tasks adults do decline in adaptability with age and that this greater rigidity applies to both physical and mental skills. The reasons seem to be partly psychological – the fear and tension that may be associated with re-training, and partly that older people have more to 'unlearn'. Their experiences are richer and more complex and may make it difficult for them to approach a new task with an open mind.

The advantages of age

On the other hand, in some subjects this richer experience obviously puts the adult at a considerable advantage, because he can fit the new information into a much more complex perceptual framework than a child. Some experiments have shown how older adults take longer to solve problems than young people. It looks as if the reasons might be that older people see greater ambiguity and complexity in intellectual or social problems than they did when younger. Experience has taught them that easy answers are to be mistrusted. Welford quotes one of his subjects, aged fifty-seven, writing after being given a problem to solve:

I find this work difficult because I am inclined to question several of the statements, instead of accepting them and drawing the conclusions, if any, which may be justly derived from them.

Welford tends to describe this adult slowness as a handicap, but it can often be a great advantage to the adult student when the teacher knows how to solicit and use the range of an adult's experience:

My most enjoyable classes have always been with the mature women students who want to take up teaching after rearing their families. They simply will not accept pat theories and glib statements about child development because all the time they are asking 'Did my children do that?' or 'Was that true when my children were four?' Whereas a twenty-year-old will write it straight down in her notebook, the mature woman always pauses to weigh and consider against her own and other people's experience. She always sees the 'ifs' and 'buts'. In these classes, by relating the students' experience to the general view, I feel we finally create a tremendously lively and complex picture of child psychology. They bring a depth and humour to rather dry theories which young people could never attain.

In situations like this, it will always be to the advantage of student and teacher if past experience can be used to the full.

Unlearning skills

However, some past experience may not be any help to an adult. A trainee learning a new manual skill may have to unlearn old skills. For instance, one might expect a woman who had experience of operating a hand sewing machine to be likely to learn quickly how to operate a power model in industry. Instead it frequently happens that she is hampered by her habit of stopping the domestic machine by hand with the hand-wheel instead of using the foot-pedal, and of trying to raise the machine-foot by hand instead of with the knee-press. Sometimes skills transfer easily enough, but at present a lot of the evidence is inconclusive, and would depend very much on which components of which skill might be appropriately compared.

Preventing and recognizing mistakes

Many adult learners find it extremely difficult to recognize that
they have made mistakes. Even when a tutor may tell them that
something is wrong they may still fail to appreciate exactly why,
or to stop themselves making identical errors over and over again.
Something like this seems to have happened to several of the
students in the dressmaking class, described with some resentful
puzzlement by this tutor:

The class I took over in mid-term consisted of fifteen 'regulars',
about half young unmarried girls, about half well over forty. After
three lessons with them I was worried as many of them were making
the same mistakes all the time and getting mad at me when I pointed
them out. One woman could not even thread the machine properly.
She *always* made mistakes, never realized she had, would start sewing, then when the thing only sewed in one thread, she'd always say,
'This dratted machine is playing up again tonight.' I'd have to go
over and tell her she'd got the threading wrong and show her how to
do it, but she always insisted that was how she had threaded it up
herself and that it was the machine that was wrong. Another woman
was very cross with me when I advised her to take out a sleeve she
had set in incorrectly (it was too puckered) because she said she
could not see anything wrong with it. In the end I took it out myself
and set it in for her, but she said it looked just the same to her. There
were another half-dozen students like this, and after a few more
lessons it became too much of a strain battling with them. Perhaps
I am a perfectionist since I trained as a tailoress in the garment industry, but I do not like to see bad work and the class closed at
Christmas when I gave it up and they could not find anyone to
replace me.

Near-open hostility like this between teacher and student is
quite rare in industry and adult education. A much more common
situation is the one where the student is willing enough to correct
mistakes if only he could identify them in the first place or
where, because a rather low standard of work is allowed, mistakes
can be innocently reinforced for years without anyone bothering
to point them out.

Correction by the teacher

In any case it would seem futile for the teacher to perform the
correction himself – he knows how to do it, it is the student who

has to learn. The error can only be put right when the student actually performs the correct response himself. Nevertheless, many teachers who rightly pride themselves on their own deft and accomplished work find a student's mistakes too painful to contemplate, and will often seize the work and do the difficult bits themselves, sometimes under the impression that students are grateful for such professional additions. There may be occasional students too placid or even too lazy to be put out in such a case, but most people feel cheated if someone else does all the hard work for them. They want the satisfaction and sense of achievement of learning to cope with the difficult parts themselves. They may find the teacher's well-meant interventions hard to endure, as in this art class run by a teacher whom the student earlier described tactfully as having 'tremendous enthusiasm but lacking method'.

General instruction is given *ad hoc* ... moreover in dealing with someone's problem, his enthusiasm leads him to paint half the picture himself, instead of merely demonstrating and suggesting and thereby letting the student feel that the picture was 'all his own work'. This makes everyone cross, but no one has had the courage to tell him we don't like it.

Misunderstandings

Frequently, though, the problem is not so much to correct errors made on the spot, but to discover what basic misunderstandings and errors from the past may still be hindering a student's progress. It would be commonplace, for instance, for an English teacher to find that a student who demands 'grammar' has no idea of what 'parts of speech' are. He has not even absorbed that words can be classified in this way. Cookery teachers constantly complain that housewives who enrol for Cordon Bleu lessons will go to elaborate lengths to conceal their ignorance of basic methods such as blending flour into butter, or at an even more fundamental level will not know how many ounces there are in a pound. Dr Belbin has commented on how, in industrial training, individuals may struggle to disguise their lack of knowledge of something simple like measurement. He says that on asking some trainees how many sixteenths they thought there were in an inch, one trainee said 'ten' and another one said 'twelve'.*

It seems from research that once mistakes have been made it is particularly hard to correct them and that the solution seems to be prevention rather than cure. Prevention in this case means making absolutely sure that on the *first* occasion of a new piece of learning the adult gets the right answer. This first occasion seems to be the really crucial one and mistakes made then are peculiarly hard to eradicate, especially if the adult makes a response he has worked out for himself.

Devising situations which make it difficult for the pupil to make mistakes can tax the teacher's ingenuity enormously. One method is described here by Anthony Cash, in a quotation from an article describing his conversion from the traditional grammatical method of teaching languages to one more solidly grounded in the needs and interests of his pupils:

Perhaps the most basic rule in language teaching is that every effort should be made to safeguard the student from mistakes. If he has heard, spoken, read and written only the correct forms he is not likely to produce the wrong ones. There is no point in asking a question if the learner cannot answer it or is likely to get the answer wrong. This means that the teacher must invent a situation about which he can pose questions to each of which there is a single and obvious answer. The following situation would give rise to a great variety of questions: 'Ivan Mikhailovich Yakalyev is a Soviet citizen working in London. Every Thursday evening he has his dinner in a Chinese restaurant in Kensington High Street.' 'Does he have dinner in the Chinese restaurant on Monday evening, Wednesday evening, Saturday evening, etc.' 'Does he have dinner in a French, Italian, Indian, etc., restaurant on Thursday evenings?' More open-ended questions would be reserved until later. 'Where does Ivan Mikhailovich have dinner on Thursdays? What does he do there?' Eventually one would ask: 'Tell me what you know about Ivan Mikhailovich Yakalyev.' When your students can tell you all about Ivan Mikhailovich Yakalyev (in speech and writing), about his family, his home, his work, his native town, his country, you do not care whether they know what the prepositional case of 'table' is.†

*R. M. Belbin, 'How do they learn?', 1969.
†Anthony Cash, 'Conversion', *Adult Education*, vol. 39, no. 6, 1967.

Giving 'knowledge of results'

Finding out straight away whether or not an answer is correct is one of the most important features of learning. Psychologists call this 'knowledge of results'. Some psychologists found that if people were asked to throw a ball over their shoulders at a target, there was no improvement if they were told nothing about how accurate or not they had been, there was some improvement if the information was delayed up to six minutes, but that there was considerable improvement if the information was given straight away.

Similar results have been found many times from other experiments, all confirming that although *some* learning can take place without knowledge of results, as F. C. Bartlett commented, 'The old saying that practice makes perfect is not true. But it is true to say that it is practice the *results of which are known* which makes perfect.'*

Translated to the classroom, these rules do seem to suggest that teachers would be well advised to develop effective and speedy means of evaluating students' work. This could take the form of a succint verbal assessment on the spot, a more elaborate and thoughtful written comment made later, or the provision of a check-list which the student could use to mark his own work. Language laboratories are useful here, as they nearly always include ways in which students can immediately check their efforts. Programmed instruction, although open to a number of objections, can be equally valuable in this way because it invites a response then tells the student straight away whether or not he is right.

Reinforcement

Obviously the learner must not come to rely too heavily on the teacher's judgement. Instead, the teacher must bring the learner to appreciate what the correct performance looks, sounds and feels like, so that eventually he can recognize for himself whether it is right or wrong. This applies as much to recognizing the quality of a good argument as to judging an artistic performance

*F. C. Bartlett, 'The measurement of human skill', *British Medical Journal*, vol. 1, 1947.

or to developing a manual skill. Most teachers recognize that frequent practice is necessary to reinforce what has been learnt and that constant reference must be made to facts or skills already taught. Perhaps this is what accounts for the frequency of that ingenuous but reasonably sound piece of advice to new teachers: 'First you tell them what you're going to tell them, then you tell them, then you tell them what you've told them.'

In some subjects, as long as the material has been logically broken up into small and easily digestible pieces, reinforcements of past material will come naturally. In languages, for instance, an advanced student is very likely to be making frequent use of the vocabulary and structures he acquired in the first few weeks of his course. In embroidery, the simple stitches are the basis of all the more elaborate ones. Advanced statistics depend on certain elementary mathematical processes used again and again, and so on. It is more difficult with subjects such as history, philosophy or sociology, where knowledge tends to be a seamless garment which has to be arbitrarily broken up into clumps, and where the relation of one fact or judgement to another is often anything but a logical progression. The problem of support in the form of explanation and reinforcement often presents intractable difficulty, not least in the amount of time available. Most teachers settle for encouraging students to look over their notes frequently, or offer two revision lessons a term, or devise a 'concentric' syllabus where general outlines of the whole subject are covered at first and then constantly revised and added to as the year goes on. Others add a quick summary of the previous lesson at the beginning of the next, or occasionally ask a member of the class to give it, although this latter method has to be used carefully. One does hear of classes where this practice has become a painful embarrassment which people arrive late to avoid, forcing the tutor eventually to discontinue the idea.

Practice

Psychologists have paid a great deal of attention to the desired length of practice periods for learning something new, and to exploring whether or not learning can be improved by taking fairly frequent rest pauses.

Timing of a break

It seems that both human and animal learning is accomplished more easily by frequent rests – estimates vary between recommending twenty-minute and forty-minute work periods, interspersed by five or ten minutes rest. In the voluntary adult-education class this is usually a question of only theoretical interest, since easily the most common pattern is a weekly two-hour session, occasionally split by a coffee break of ten or fifteen minutes. Added to that, most adult education happens in the evening when students and teachers are likely to be tired after a full day's work. Common experience shows how extremely welcome some kind of break is, even if it is only a five-minute pause for pacing the corridor outside with a cigarette, or having a chat with a friend. Many teachers also place a high value on a coffee break as a time when students are less shy, and when real and valuable friendships can develop among the group or between members of different groups.

In industry, where more flexible periods of time are available, it is more likely that there will be opportunities for manipulating the length of practice periods to suit the trainees. Here the evidence certainly suggests that spaced practice may be better for manual skills, particularly at the initial stages. If learning becomes too concentrated the trainee either shows no improvement or else actually does worse than he was doing originally. After a rest his performance may go up to a higher level than he previously achieved. However, Eunice Belbin has shown that for older people on industrial-training schemes long periods of practice may be very much more appropriate – not only did the trainees in her experiment prefer a long practice period without a break, they also made startlingly better progress when allowed to learn in this way.* For younger people short initial practice periods of half an hour may be more suitable, followed by two-hour sessions at later stages.

'Whole' or 'part' method

Much attention has also been paid to whether 'whole' or 'part' methods are better for learning. The 'whole' method would in-

*Eunice Belbin, 'Training the adult worker', *Problems of Progress in Industry*, no. 15, HMSO, 1964.

A.L.—4

volve learning a complete job all at once without attempting to learn successive stages one at a time. Supporters of this method believe that divisions between parts of a task are often arbitrary, and that in practice a skilled operator performs his task as *one* movement or series of movements. In industry now this is coming to be a matter of little significance, as there are fewer 'whole' jobs which have to be learnt and in practice most training is done by the 'cumulative-part method' – in other words the task is learnt by parts but these are constantly revised as new 'units' are added on.

Eyes and ears

Hearing and vision both start declining in efficiency quite early in life – indeed it has been estimated that sight is at its best at the age of ten, that 'long-sightedness' is increasingly likely to set in very gradually after then, and that at about forty there is likely to be an accelerating decline in visual 'acuity' (the ability to perceive fine detail): the size of the pupil decreases considerably and there is a slowing down of adaptation to the dark. In hearing there is an equally noticeable deterioration. Hearing is probably at its best at about the age of fifteen or sixteen and decline starts after about twenty. Between the years of twenty and forty there is a loss of about 10 per cent in the capacity to hear the high sound frequencies.

Practical improvements

A few simple recognitions of these facts can make enormous practical improvements to a class of adults. For instance, the room should be well-lit (not always easy to achieve in the dim illumination often provided in rooms meant primarily for the hardier eyes of children) and free from glare; blackboard work should be easy to read; grubby grey blackboards where it is difficult to distinguish chalk from board should be avoided. Textbooks and typed materials should have large print, so that reading from them is easy. People with poor sight should be quietly encouraged to sit near the front if visual material is being used. If a television programme is incorporated into the lesson the set should be correctly tuned with the contrast as sharp as possible. If the students are sitting in rows this may make it difficult for someone at the back to hear another student who speaks from the front: circular seating arrangements are better – older people with poor hearing often need to *see* that another person is speaking because speech alone does not attract their attention. Students should be encouraged to speak slowly and clearly and to complain if they cannot hear. The acoustics of a room can often be improved by drawing curtains.

Learning to learn

Finally, can adults learn to learn? Can their ability to learn be improved? All the evidence shows that the answer to both these questions is Yes. Industrial experience shows the importance of continued practice – trainees who have engaged in some form of keeping educationally in trim since leaving school consistently do better than those who have had no such practice, even if the 'practice' has no immediate relevance to the training itself. It follows that adults who can gain confidence in learning through undertaking a well-planned course suited to their needs will improve not only in the skills they have come to learn, but can also be expected to improve in the skills of actually learning how to learn. It seems, too, that adults can usefully be given some insight into how the learning process operates, particularly when they are students who have not had any formal education for a number of years. Often this is given as an introductory session to apprehensive novices, and is called something like 'How to Study'; it would include simple pieces of advice and practice on taking notes, spacing practice-periods, using libraries and so on.

Learning experiments

Some teachers feel that this in itself is not enough – they like their students to participate in a 'learning experiment' so that they can experience for themselves how the general pattern of learning works. In the classroom experience described below, the training officer hit on his method not out of careful thought and planning, but in a moment of inspiration produced by the extra-vagant despair of his trainees. (The 'learning curve' refers to a typical result of drawing a graph to plot improvement in perfor-mance with practice, which usually shows a rapid initial improvement, followed by a 'plateau' or stage of little or no progress, and finally a considerable improvement.)

About two years ago I had a group of intelligent women trainees who suddenly decided they were not making fast enough progress. They had had an excellent beginning, but most of them were finding the harder work very tough. They began to act worried, then to nag me and finally they were all threatening to leave. There was a jokey atmosphere on the surface, but they were three-quarters serious. I think now that we should have modified the scheme earlier in various ways, but at the time I was racking my brains for immediate solutions when I suddenly thought of the learning curves I'd learned about on *my* training course. The next day they all had pieces of paper, rulers and pencils waiting for them on their tables. They were completely mystified, more so when I asked them each to produce a small pocket mirror from their handbags, and to divide into pairs. I then explained that we were going to see for ourselves how learning works by constructing our own learning curves. One woman in each pair acted as recorder, and drew the two axes on the graph paper, one for number of trials and one for 'time taken' in minutes. The task was to prop the mirror up on the paper and looking only in the mirror to write the name of the firm so that it read correctly in the mirror. Of course this is quite difficult, but not too difficult and they thoroughly enjoyed doing it. After fifteen minutes I gathered in all the graphs, and sure enough, all of them showed the same pattern. We discussed this and then went on with comparing the performances of those who had only watched and recorded on the first run, comparing results after a rest, and so on and so on, and in this way the trainees discovered for themselves the general pattern a practice curve forms, and it was not long before they were relating this to their own experience on the course and recognizing their difficulties for what they were – 'plateaux' in the learning process. I considered the mirror exercise to be so valuable that I always incorporate it now into our first sessions with new groups of fair intelligence like this one.

This would not be everyone's choice of method, nor would it work with every sort of group, especially if there were individuals in it who did not know how to plot a graph. Nevertheless, adults are usually grateful for some help in understanding learning, though tutors should be careful about presenting such a course to mature students who may resent the implication that they need to learn how to learn.

It should go without saying that courses on 'how to study' should follow the same principles of good teaching as every other type of course. It would be no use *telling* students how to make notes or use a library. As with every other skill, they can only learn by finding out and practising it for themselves.

Chapter 4
Teachers and their Groups

I admit to feeling some considerable panic as the time for the first class meeting approached. I was not at all sure what to expect but I was afraid that what I might find was twenty-five intellectual giants. How on earth was I to behave? I didn't have a clue.

Although I had had considerable experience of adult education in London, I was very dubious when asked to teach here, as it is a rural area where everybody knows everybody, and I knew that a large number of my 'students' would be people I already knew well in other ways. I anticipated some difficulty in establishing myself as 'teacher' with people who were on sherry-party terms with me and my family.

It was with mixed feeling of apprehension and pleasant anticipation that I looked forward to my new class at the adult centre. I had enjoyed all my teaching there before, liking the friendly atmosphere and the good relationships with my class, but on this occasion I wished to introduce some revolutionary methods and was not unworried about how my new students would react. If they took against the method then my belief in class democracy would oblige me to return to what I now considered to be the bad old ways.

Previous chapters have looked at some of the problems and backgrounds of the individual adult learner; this chapter is about the teacher, the alternative styles of teaching open to him, the pressures upon him; it is also about the sum of those individual learners plus teacher that go to make up and influence the adult group.

The teacher's anxieties

As some of the quotations above show, problems of anxiety and uncertainty are not limited to the learner in teaching adults. In his way the teacher, particularly if he is inexperienced, is just as likely to feel nervous. He will be concerned about whether he is, say, a good enough sociologist, or an expert enough linguist to meet the demands of his students (plenty of adult teachers are terrified of being found out as charlatans). He will be worried about method – will it be appropriate to teach industrial relations only by lecture plus discussion? Will it be the right thing to teach design by using a discussion plus television series? He will be worried about the likely standards of his students and about how he is to teach individual students of widely ranging abilities and to evaluate their work sensibly. He will be worried about exactly what sort of personal teaching – learning relationship is either possible or ideal.

Schoolteachers who also teach adults often find this a particularly pressing problem. In school a teacher may feel no uncertainty about how to behave with the children. He is always older than they are, frequently their intellectual superior, has the advantage of a longer education, and can lean heavily on an established authority structure and tradition which is familiar to everyone. Even a sixth-form teacher faced with an unusually bright and mature set of pupils can take some comfort in his longer and 'superior' experience. Not so the teacher of adults. He may be younger than all his students, he may even be less intelligent; there is no familiar system or tradition to work in; he may be totally isolated from colleagues; he may have had no training whatever in teaching; the only distinguishing mark between himself and his students may be the particular expertise he has in his subject. As the keep-fit teacher comments in a survey by W. E. Styler, she found one of her main difficulties was 'being unable to order them like children, but having to suggest instruction in such a way as to command their respect and attention'.* Other teachers with less of the military in their vocabulary are familiar with the same problem: how does one achieve the right mix of deference to the fact that the students are fellow adults, but still retain their leadership in order to teach them?

The teacher's influence

Certainly it seems that the teacher is the most important single element in setting the style of a class, as great or even a greater influence on the whole occasion that the sum of all the other individuals. This will come as no surprise to experienced teachers,

*W. E. Styler, 'Further education: part-time teachers speak', University of Hull, 1968.

who will have noticed with dismay how even with a group of apparently stable and self-possessed adults who contribute a good deal to an active discussion, their own moods of exhilaration, pleasure, boredom or irritation are invariably conveyed to a class, and that these reflections from their own personality are in some degree returned as mirror images in the way students behave to them and to each other.

Compare for instance the atmosphere in the classroom and the response by students in two highly contrasted classes in the same institute. The groups were observed and then described in a report by the former principal of the institute, Ivy Cooper Marsh.

The French class (students all roughly the same age, in their early 30s). He is a conscientious and knowledgeable man and, if he were not so rigid and traditional in his methods, his classes would be more enjoyable for the students and he would be able to keep the interests of a wider range of ages and abilities. This tutor is clearly not a tutor to meet the challenge of heterogeneity. He tends to use 'school' methods and to expect students to learn by rote, a routine ' 'ults find unacceptable. ... Everything stems from the teacher and 'en when he was encouraged to have a circle of chairs, the tutor continued to keep the atmosphere formal. The activity of the student is boringly the same – repetition of words and phrases. The students admire him but find him formidable in spite of his good nature. ... There is no feeling in his classes of a group of *adults* engaged in a common project, and no incentive to widen horizons and learn to manage on their own when class attendance ceases, as it must at some time.

This tutor has repeatedly deplored the fact that without examinations you cannot get good standards or measure what you have done.

The fishing-rod-making class (students of widely varying ages). It would seem to be an excellent example of an unobtrusive teacher nevertheless emanating an atmosphere of competence, confidence and enthusiasm which produces in the learners the maximum effect and group goodwill. ...

He is a quiet man and there is absolutely no obvious domination of the class – indeed going into the workshop it is difficult to pick out the tutor – there are groups here and there discussing their work and helping one another. There is a feeling of interest and industry in the class generally and the atmosphere is relaxed. Any one of the students was willing to talk about what his neighbour was doing ... most students coming to this class know what they want to do, but the teacher is constantly showing them new materials and new methods.

He has his own retail business and himself keeps abreast of innovations. In this manner he is authoritative on his subject – also a skilful craftsman himself – his students admire and respect his expertise. He has a wide interest around his craft and gives his students every benefit of this. Very old rods, which occasionally come his way, he brings in for his students to make comparisons with new types, and I have seen some old worthwhile rods being beautifully repaired and renovated by students in this class. In this way he is teaching his students to recognize good materials and expert workmanship and to admire and emulate such things.*

Even allowing for the differences in subject and students and for the personal preferences of the observer, it is clear that very different teaching styles were being used. In consequence the results each teacher was likely to achieve were deeply affected. The French teacher's formidable and rigorous drilling appealed to the highly motivated, fairly able students. The others (about half the initial enrolment) dropped out early in the term. Everything about this teacher's style emphasized the students' dependence on him; he was the sole source of information, and it is perhaps significant that he used no audio-visual aids (apart from a textbook). This sort of teacher undoubtedly gets good results with those who can survive his regime, but even then he himself feels that it is only by applying the external sanctions of examinations that students will work.

In the rod-making class, on the other hand, although there is perhaps a smaller work output, it is difficult to distinguish the teacher from anyone else at first. Instead of communication being limited to student to teacher, teacher to student, there is constant flow of comment and discussion between tutor and students, and students among themselves, and a feeling that the students are being encouraged to take responsibility themselves for what and how much they are learning.

Teaching styles and group theories

There has been a good deal of research on how a 'leader' affects his group, and one hopes that many of the results are relevant to the adult teacher and his class. Even so, research can only sug-

*Ivy Cooper Marsh, 'Adult students: an inquiry into how and why they learn', Eltham Adult Education Institute, 1969.

gest, and every suggestion must be hedged with 'perhaps', 'but' or 'maybe'. Neither in England nor America has there been large-scale, meticulous, disinterested and painstaking research into actual adult classes. The adult teacher looking for guidance is obliged to pick up crumbs from here and there and to hope that there will be something of relevance to his classroom. A colleague of mine once sadly remarked that the records of classwork which our college valued so highly were much more records of what he wished he had done with his classes than what he had actually done. Similarly, some of this research, because it has been done outside the classroom and particularly outside the adult classroom, might well be what one hopes might be true and applicable rather than what actually is.

Another qualification must be that small-group research has been to some psychologists a kind of substitute religion. Many experimenters seem to have been anxious to demonstrate the moral superiority of one kind of group or a method of leading a group over another, and this has undoubtedly coloured their results. It is clearly difficult to devise experiments involving human groups, since each group, its situation, and the task it is set, will vary as much as individuals vary. Some of the experiments done on groups have been made under laboratory conditions, involving procedures so unfair or so wildly unlikely to elicit realistic behaviour from the subjects that the results must remain suspect. In one experiment, designed to test group organization and cooperation, the experimenter made an excuse to leave the room, locked the group in, then sent fake smoke pouring under the door while a fire alarm sounded in the building and the experimenters watched their victims smugly and safely from behind a one-way mirror in the ceiling.

Types of leadership

Nevertheless such prankishness is comparatively rare, and social psychology has usefully suggested some general rules, particularly on styles of leadership, which have some relevance to teacher behaviour. In one of the most often quoted field studies of a type initiated by Kurt Lewin and his followers in the 1930s, the behaviour of three different types of leadership was observed. Matched groups of ten-year-old boys in youth clubs were in turn placed under three different types of leadership: 'authoritarian', where the leader was stern, bossy, encouraged competitiveness, punished those who misbehaved, and made all the important decisions himself; *'laissez-faire'*, where he did virtually nothing – for instance, he remained withdrawn from the boys unless he was directly asked a question; and democratic, where the children themselves decided what they would do, and regarded the leader as someone who could help individuals where necessary and who laid stress on individual solutions of problems. All three leaders set the groups on various handicraft tasks. In the authoritarian groups the boys were submissive and well behaved on the surface while the leader was present, but showed signs even then of submerged aggression, often 'mishearing' instructions or 'accidentally' damaging materials. Amongst themselves they were competitive and mutually disparaging. When the leader left the room they tended to abandon work instantly and to run about noisily. The *laissez-faire* groups did almost no work at all whether or not the leader was present. Under democratic leadership the boys worked well together without fear of one outdoing the other, there was little tension or aggression in the atmosphere, and unlike the boys from the authoritarian group, some of whom broke up their models at the end of the course, all the work was regarded as 'ours' and treasured accordingly. The temporary absence of the leader made no difference to the amount of work the boys did.

Many people have questioned how far these results can be expected to apply to other situations, but this study remains a classic of its kind, especially as it shows that the *same boys behaved differently with each leader.* Subsequent laboratory experiments and field studies with adults have repeatedly shown that a friendly, understanding leader or teacher who encourages members to take active part in events, including taking responsibility for procedural decisions (like when to have a break, or whether or not to smoke), will greatly improve the effectiveness of the group, producing greater spontaneity, and more initiative from individual members. Dominant, aloof, authoritarian teachers tend to produce either very hostile or very subdued group members. Where actual learning is measured, the authoritarian-style group may produce more if what is being learnt is straightforward, with only one type of 'right' answer encouraged. On the other hand, where a change of attitude is involved, as it usually is in most WEA or university extra-mural departments, the 'participating' group is clearly superior.

There is some evidence, too, that creativity is more strongly encouraged in groups where the teacher does not dominate, and a good deal of evidence that the participatory group is the one most people prefer, perhaps because this is the type of group where pleasant social relationships are most likely to develop. The more people talk to one another, the more inclined they are to like one another. It is clearly much easier to retain an irrational dislike for someone you hardly ever talk to than for someone with whom you frequently discuss and argue. Teachers should not forget that such relationships are important to students. Many teachers tend to be innocent of any knowledge of what the relationships are between their students because they think only in terms of students' relationship with themselves.

Working in groups

Some work has also been done on the effects of deliberate competition both between different groups and between individuals. For instance, in one experiment a class of students was divided into two to discuss problems; one group was told that individual contributions made in the group would count towards their course marks, the other group was told that it was the group score which would count. In the competitive group the students were not really interested in what other people said, not friendly to one another, and produced stereotyped answers. In the cooperative group the students enjoyed themselves more, produced a greater variety of solutions, and were relaxed and friendly towards each other.

There has also been a good deal of general research into how small groups solve problems, with the idea of finding out whether it is truer to say that many hands make light work rather than that too many cooks spoil the broth. Common sense dictates that this will depend on what the problem is, and that it will also depend on what range of intelligence or experience is available in the group, as well as on who decides whether one solution is 'better' than another. Research here has tended to confirm that on tasks such as crossword puzzles or mathematics which demand concentrated individual attention with only one right answer, individual solutions can be reached quicker than group ones. But on problems, say, of politics, human relations, philosophy or the performing arts, or any subject where there might be any number of solutions, a group of people produces a far more varied and stimulating range of ideas than an individual.

One must remember, too, that the cooperative group can become a powerful mechanism for encouraging individuals to feats they could never manage on their own. Alcoholics Anonymous is one well-known example, Weight Watchers is another. In both these organizations people who by themselves have failed over a number of years to cure their addiction have achieved astonishing successes with the help of a group. In teaching terms, many students who have struggled on their own with a subject can find new strength from a group, even if the skill they are learning is essentially – like solo singing, for instance – an individual activity. Perhaps this is just as Thomas à Kempis said, that 'it is the solace of the wretched to have companions in their misery', or perhaps the group really does have a dynamic effect on individual capabilities.

Implications for the classroom

What is the sum of all this research? What are the alternatives for teachers? One way of looking at the situation is to suggest two deliberate extremes in classroom terms: the democratic or student-centred group, and the authoritarian or teacher-centred group. Here are some of the implications:

In the student-centred group members will have discussed the aims of the course and will have themselves decided what methods are to be adopted. In the class itself there will be a constant exchange of ideas between student and student and a high degree of individual activity and cooperation on the part of each student, whether this is discussion or creative craft tasks. Such a group will contain members at many different levels of skill and intelligence who can work together satisfactorily. The teacher's role in this sort of group will be to protect and encourage individual members, to develop a high degree of sensitivity and expertise in interpreting the feelings of the group, and to be seen by them primarily as a teacher rather than as a subject expert. In many ways the teacher becomes just another member of the group. The main criterion of success in such a group is that a student will feel able by the end of the course to go on learning on his own – that he has become a person capable of planning and extending his own learning.

In the teacher-centred group, on the other hand, the teacher will decide the aim of the course and will expect the students to conform to them. Those who cannot conform will tend to drop out or be made to feel uncomfortable if they stay. The teacher himself will do most of the talking, and if there is any discussion it will tend to take the form of student to teacher or teacher to student, rather than between student and student. The teacher will tend to see students as a remote mass rather than as individuals, and will dismiss the idea that he might hurt or discourage them by his comments, or lack of them. He will emphasize his remoteness from the group by sitting apart from them and by refusing or finding it difficult to mix with students on equal terms or to admit to ignorance or to having made a mistake. He will encourage competition between students. There will be frequent use of tests and examinations to grade and assess students, resulting in a group where the students are streamed by ability, and where only the able students survive because the teacher finds it impossible to cope with different standards of ability in the group. Students will become completely passive and dependent on the teacher as the source of all information and are unlikely to develop much on their own.

This is, of course, a caricature of two extremes in teaching styles. In practice I have never seen a class in adult education dominated by so unpleasant a creature as the second type of teacher, nor have I ever seen a group that was as democratic as the first type. (Even so, the French class and the rod-making class described earlier in this chapter show that startling contrasts along these lines do exist in teacher style.) It is more useful, perhaps, to see each extreme as the opposite ends of a continuum, a line of possible teaching styles which blend imperceptibly into one another. Most teachers would probably try to aim for something between the extremely authoritarian and the extremely democratic group, depending on their own personalities and on the wishes and personalities of their students.

In any case, in adult education, and to some extent in industrial training too, there is a tradition of student participation in classes to which most tutors would pay lip service. It would be hard to find a teacher who did not at least believe in student participation as an ideal. But applying an ideal in practice can prove tricky. It is with these and related difficulties in group management that the next section is concerned.

Difficulties

I could have stood on my head in that class for all the reaction I'd have got. I often felt like coming in with a false moustache or a clown's nose to see if it would even have surprised them. Personally I participated like mad, they never did.

How can you get a good discussion going with forty large adults who sit in a room designed for twenty small children?

The hardest thing is to shut up and *listen*. I know I talk too much, but at school you have to, to survive, and it is hard to kick the habit with the adult class. I always try to remind myself that the things I remember best from the class I go to are the things I personally say. That helps me to keep my mouth closed.

A teacher who wants to encourage greater group particpation will find several sources of difficulty: his own personality and the extent to which he is able to step back from the limelight, or even to be objective about his own role in the class; the external pressures of the institution or community; administrative pressures which may keep groups too large for effective participation; and the pressures that may come from the students themselves to keep proceedings formal.

The teacher's temperament

I was once myself a member of a class in seventeenth-century drama which was taken by a teacher of some local academic fame who frequently told us that he was committed to full participation by students in the process of learning, that our learning was to be a mutually cooperative venture, and that he expected to learn as much himself from the class as we did. In fact, although a person of considerable wit and charm, he also had such an autocratic and impetuous temperament that he talked most of the time himself, answered at least half his own questions because he could not tolerate the potential embarrassment of a silence, and occasionally conducted what were indeed vigorous and searching discussions, but always with the same three or four most naturally voluble and perhaps most able students. He made a few token efforts to coax speech out of the others, but gave the impression that he probably never noticed how little they responded. By the end of a ten-week course the numbers had reduced to below half the original large enrolment, and even among the survivors there were two people who did not utter a single word in twenty hours of class contact.

One piece of research has confirmed how little teachers may know objectively of their own part in lessons. Alvin Zander made a study of four teachers of adults who claimed to be committed to student participation, and found that on average they lectured for 27 per cent of the time, matched each student's contribution with one of their own, and made nine out of ten of all the procedural decisions.* Other research has tended to show how teachers may have no idea how much attention they are paying to particular students. In one study of a class of twenty-six, the teacher was found to be giving more than a quarter of his attention to the well-adjusted pupils who presumably did not need it. Even after he had realized this, he found it extremely difficult to distribute his attention more fairly.† Many teachers will recognize it as a familiar temptation to go on encouraging those who need little encouragement, and to avoid the difficult and perhaps painful or embarrassing job of helping those who may be silent, moody or unstable.

Many teachers may feel obliged because of the present educational climate to make progressive noises about how much

* Alvin Zander, 'Student motives and teaching methods in four informal adult classes', *Adult Education USA*, vol. 2, 1951.

† J. Withall, 'An objective measure of a teacher's classroom interactions', *Journal of Educational Research*, vol. 47, 1956.

'participation' goes on in their classes, but once the classroom door is closed they may revert to the more dominant style they really prefer, and perhaps are better suited to by temperament, experience or expectation. It is not only the students who bring certain stereotyped expectations with them; teachers are equally subject to the forces of tradition, and the older adult tutor is as likely as his older student to have been educated when one was not considered to be teaching in a classroom unless one was talking a good deal of the time oneself. It is not surprising, too, that some adult tutors, particularly well qualified ones who have got to the top by lectures and reading alone, are inclined to think that what was good enough for them is good enough for their classes.

This particular difficulty does not only apply to older tutors. Many young people come straight into some occasional teaching of adults from having recently completed their own university education. Bearing in mind the current competition for university places it is likely that most of their own education will have been of a highly academic sort, much of it consisting of rigid and formalized teaching which even a teacher-training course does little to modify. Simple inexperience and uncertainty may lead these young teachers into attempting to simulate with the adult class the kind of teaching with which they themselves have been most familiar. Many of them find themselves in the odd situation of being the youngest person in the classroom, yet being the person who is expected to take the lead. This is a complete reversal of the educational situation most of them have been in for sixteen years of their lives. Many will confidently assume that it will be all right to use the same kind of modern approach they may be using with children, and will rightly rely on honestly admitting their limitations, and on the kindness of the class, to protect them from their own absurdities. Others may retreat through panic into lofty formality rather than face the hazardous excitements of a more relaxed approach.

Pressures from outside

Sometimes tutors will use the supposed wishes of the students or the supposed traditions of the institution as an excuse for dominating the class. The argument then goes something like, 'Of course the students are too dim (or too shy, or too noisy) to take much real part in things', or 'They *want* you to be in charge', or, more subtly, 'Of course we'd like to run things on a participatory basis but the principal prefers the traditional approach.'

Many of these alibis contain considerable elements of truth. Institutions, or even those outside them, may exert direct or indirect pressure on teachers. For instance it would not be unusual, in a college of further education running day-release courses for young apprentices from a particular firm, for someone from the firm to telephone the principal to say that he thoroughly disapproved of all this discussion and poetry that his lads were getting up to on Wednesday afternoons, that they were being sent to the college to learn engineering, and if they did English then it ought to be engineering English. Pressures may not be so direct in adult education but they are there, and frequently exerted in gentler ways. 'I'm afraid the noise from your discussion group upset my class, Mr Smith,' or, 'The local newspaper has got hold of your class social survey. They say people are complaining about answering intimate questions. Perhaps you'd better get them to stop for this week', and so on.

The size of the group

One of the most useful and yet at the same time, once pointed out, most obvious findings from small-group research has been that the larger the group, the fewer the people who speak. In a class of only six people, everyone will most probably speak. If that class is doubled and then trebled, a progressively smaller proportion will open their mouths at all. The group becomes dominated by a few voluble and confident members, and the others are silenced. It would be quite commonplace to find that, in a class of eighteen, most of the talking was done by four or five people, including the teacher. It seems to be a basic law of group life that individual contributions vary negatively with group size, and it does not take any great psychological insight to see why; particularly if there is only a short period of time available, not everyone would feel bold enough to say a great deal in front of a lot of other people. The ideal size for groups is probably between eight and twelve (depending on the subject), as this number provides enough productive people to make discussion interesting without being so big that it inhibits individuals too much from talking. But since many adult-education and industrial-training classes are and must for administrative convenience be larger than a dozen, it is one of the tutor's constant headaches to devise ways of breaking the pattern in which discussion and attention is left to and given to only a few members.

In discussing this problem in adult education and industrial training it is often assumed that 'the silent member', 'the over-talkative member' or 'the know-all' can somehow be swatted down or coaxed along with a few tactful words from the teacher. Usually the advice given to teachers or group leaders assumes that he will maintain a god-like role in issuing generous praise, a few quiet appeals to better nature, or some well-calculated rudeness where necessary. This approach nearly always seems to fail. It is true that the teacher is inevitably the person with most control over classroom atmosphere and procedures, but if talking in a well-established group is being left to one or two people only, then there is something radically wrong with the group which is not curable by superficial encouragements or discouragements aimed at individual members. In a group where there is a high level of participation, responsibility for procedures and controls will be shared among members, and it will be quite usual for students themselves to encourage those who are shy, or to be more ruthless than a teacher might care to be in silencing the garrulous. For instance, in the following extract from a description of an obviously enjoyable literature class of highly motivated and hard-working students, the teacher comments thankfully on the way that this role was assumed by the only man in her group:

We had a verbose housewife who was given to endless personal reminiscing. Fortunately there was one very bluff outspoken male member of the class who would interrupt her incessant flow with, 'That's enough, Mrs P. Give the rest of us a look-in!' adding some good-natured quip. She fortunately took such interruptions in good part and was always prepared to laugh at her own absurdities.

This sort of check would be unthinkable in any but a group which had accepted that they were involved in a totally cooperative task. Where this is not the case and where the teacher is finding considerable difficulties in group control, the outward symptoms – uneven participation by members, restlessness or doziness, formally arranged furniture and so on – are usually a sign that the group's resources in materials, opinions and stimulus are too limited. The possible solutions will vary according to the type of subject, but the most successful will take the spotlight away from the teacher *during class time* and put the emphasis on many different sources of information (the students' own experience, a radio tape, books, photographs, work cards) which the teacher coordinates and directs but does not dominate.

A related difficulty in a large class is that once a group has broken down its original barriers of reserve, the problem may be that too many people rather than too few want to speak. At one conference I attended so many members of a group of nine were clamouring to speak at once that one eminent delegate was heard to say in exasperation that he was unable to discuss the topic any more – the only way he could talk about it was by giving a lecture. As a group develops, more and more members may suffer from the highly understandable feeling that if only everyone else would shut up they could deliver individually a perfect solution to whatever is under discussion. A group which has reached this intense and involved stage can readily use such a feeling in a constructive way by inviting individuals to deliver papers or to lead the discussion themselves.

Many such solutions will involve splitting the group into several small groups, whether this is for craft work in a design class, or small discussion groups in a sociology class. In a discussion-based class this splitting up has to be done with care. It is very often a most effective way of increasing individual contributions, but it can look like a stale, manipulative device, an application of group-dynamics theories for the sake of applying the theory rather than because it answers students' needs.

The wishes of students

I once sat in on an industrial-relations course with a group of eighteen men, who were using an elegant room well equipped for small-group work, with special tables and close carpeting to deaden noise. The small-group discussion came at the end of a tiring day's work, and consisted mostly of listening to lectures, with half an hour for discussion afterwards. It was clear that in their three small groups they were feeling disgruntled and had felt that they were groping for direction, even though they dutifully exchanged experiences and all spoke a great deal. After several weeks of going along with the teacher they asked for *whole*-group discussion, as they said they felt they could benefit more from the exchange of views amongst the whole group than they could in groups of six. Perhaps this was a more ambiguous situation than it at first appeared : the teacher was taking no part at all in the small-group work, but spent this part of the class 'marking the register' (having a rest). Neither was there any reporting-back session. The afternoon ended when the small groups broke up, and it was possible to discern amongst the students some dissatisfaction with the teacher's obvious disengagement – he didn't seem to care, so why should they? Maybe their attempt to resume whole-group work (which involved the teacher becoming group leader again) was simply an attempt to force him to do what they thought was his job.

This idea of ambiguous and ambivalent behaviour between groups and teachers is fascinating but difficult territory to explore, because the whole subject is inevitably and endlessly speculative. For instance, when a group pleads with a teacher to give them a lecture, who is to say whether they are doing so because they have all genuinely reached the stage where they need the information a lecture can conveniently and neatly provide, or whether they are asking for a lecture because it makes fewer demands on them than working on a project, or reading a book.

Some group theorists, admittedly drawing largely on experiences with therapy groups of mentally disturbed patients in clinics, have suggested that groups have an unconscious life of their own, and that if a group finds its set task unpleasant or difficult it will retreat into diversionary activities of its own.* At its most obvious, this would explain the ingenuity shown by schoolchildren in devising delicious red herrings as a diversionary trap for a teacher who is preparing to give them a test; or, at a less obvious level, it could explain the situation where a great deal of a lesson is taken up in conversation or argument between a teacher and a favourite pupil, while everybody else sits back and lets them get on with it.

* For example, W. R. Bion, *Experience in Groups*, Tavistock, 1961.

The charismatic teacher

Certainly 'dependance' on teachers is frequently observed in adult-education classes. Indeed in one book what amounts to dependance is held up as a model. A. J. Ratcliffe suggests that there are two patterns for the ideal adult tutor: 'the man of method', who can reduce everything to organized simplicities; and 'the man of charm', whose students actually beg him to continue – 'I could listen to you all day though you were only repeating nonsense syllables.' *

Students may quite consciously exert pressure to keep a teacher in this performing role. Whether or not this is 'dependant' behaviour in Bion's terms, and whether or not a tutor goes along with theories of unconscious urges in groups, it is often the case that although students may agree in theory that discussion and participation is a splendid thing, they may in practice feel cheated, shy or indignant if they find that they are expected to play a fully active part in the group themselves and to take full responsibility for their own learning – surely the ultimate aim of all education. They *want* a great sage, they *want* to admire the teacher, to turn him into some kind of god, and they may try by flattery, threat, discontent and restlessness to force the teacher into doing what they want. Unfortunately there is a strong tradition in adult education, as strong as its opposite of student participation, which encourages this sort of relationship. Richard Hoggart puts it succinctly, stressing the attractiveness of this easy trap for the teacher:

The urge towards a generalized charismatic relationship, that way of showing off one's own personality which ends in the rhetoric of a lay preacher, is the strongest of all temptations. You have to learn to suspect those evenings when you feel a throb come into your voice, your eye seems bright and eager, and the students look up at you with a touch of wondering admiration. Two types of teacher – in any kind of education, but adult education is a specially dangerous area in these ways – should be particularly suspected: the charismatic, an imaginative pied piper of Hamelin; and the systems builder, an intellectual pied piper of Hamelin, who offers a complete guide

* A. J. Ratcliffe, *The Adult Class: An Outline of Teaching Practice*, Nelson, 1945.

and system to experience. Men who are a combination of both – some types of Marxist are like that – are the most dubious. Any teacher who begins to acquire fans, disciples, followers, ought to suspect himself until he has examined as honestly as he can the nature of these relationships. He may well be getting between the students and their own hold on the subject. We should be glad to be judged by the degree to which our students stand on their own feet, out of our shadows. Which means we have to try to make sure they retain their freedom to be critical of us. Or, if that sounds too grand, ironic about us and towards us.*

A teacher talented in the dangerous hypnotic way Hoggart describes can easily turn his class into an audience for a personal performance. Often when students praise a teacher for being 'a good lecturer', what they mean is that he is a stimulating *performer*, by turns clown, tragedian, preacher, rhetoritician, who rouses emotions at the time but leaves nothing for students to do themselves. This is not only a danger to the intellectual. Craft teachers suffer just the same sort of temptation to show off their expertise, only of course the 'performance' will take the form of a demonstration. In such cases a large part of the lesson will be taken up in a flawless demonstration by the teacher, which students are often quite happy to encourage.

Social problems of groups

Sometimes the problem is not so much any unconscious 'dependant' urges the students may have, but simply that students are shy, or unused to the kind of group where everyone is expected to join in. In these circumstances some teachers will help the process along by using *social* participation first – thus one person's job will be to mark the register, another's will be to round up absentees, yet another's will be to set up the slide projector or put the kettle on for the coffee. Singling people out for such mild tasks can be a useful way of breaking the ice, and some tutors would claim that it is only a small step from setting up the slide projector to bringing a few slides from home to show to the rest of the class, and thereby demonstrating that the teacher has no monopoly of resources and wisdom.

* Richard Hoggart, 'The role of the teacher', in J. Rogers (ed.), *Teaching on Equal Terms*, BBC Publications, 1969.

Very occasionally serious questions of control arise in an adult group. It is true that there is never a 'discipline problem' as there can be in teaching schoolchildren; since no adult education is compulsory, a dignified exit is always possible for the disgruntled teacher or student. Nevertheless, unpleasant situations do develop now and then, as in this drama group:

I was in my second week with a group which I had taken over from an established producer. They all knew one another very well and resented me (they were always talking about how marvellous my predecessor was). I was attempting to audition them to cast a play and to keep a general discussion going at the same time, but all the way through one woman talked in a very loud voice and tried to get a little group going round her. In the end I had to speak to her sharply, but she did not stop. I tried taking her to one side but that failed. I tried flattering her by giving her a good part, but that failed, she still sabotaged my lesson by talking when it was not her turn. Fortunately she gave up in the end and left, taking her cronies with her.

Here, as in most of these cases, it would seem that the key to analysing why the situation developed as it did is in the teacher's statement that she had taken over the group from someone else. One hears of similar occasions, where a group which has been running for several years and has achieved a life of intense value to its members will bitterly resent any change of leadership, and will attempt, often successfully, to freeze out a newcomer. There is little a teacher can do here except to refrain from criticizing his predecessor, to refuse to imitate him, and to hope that in time the group will accept that it can proceed just as satisfactorily in a slightly different direction.

Two provisos must be added here. Firstly, whatever the difficulty, there are no pat solutions. I am always suspicious of those descriptions of teaching situations which start by describing some appalling class which is miraculously made first a little better, then at last totally transformed by the application of some simple theory. Teaching and learning is not a simple process; each group and each teacher is unique. Procedures which seem workable by one teacher and one group will not satisfy another.

Secondly, adult groups do not, of course, inevitably pose one painful problem after another. The majority coast along quite happily, taking small difficulties in their stride. Some classes and teachers continue serenely for many years, others become, even in a short time, powerful and vigorous social units whose members are willing to extend formal class time to take in weekend excursions, visits, courses at residential colleges or evening theatre trips, and develop close friendships which will outlast the class. At a less intense level, it would be quite normal to find that about half the classes at any evening institute had found some way to organize an end-of-term party which both involved the teacher as just another member and at the same time made some ritual gesture towards celebrating his special status.

Best of all we had an end-of-session party to which we all contributed food and drink. Very enjoyable it was too! This was an unofficial meeting in our own time, but just before the end Mr R., who had spent most of the year making ribald jokes at my expense, presented me with an elaborately wrapped parcel containing an enormous box of chocolates and, on top, a beautifully written 'poem' dedicated to the group and listing in doggerel verse the various idiosyncrasies of the members – including one lady's habit of doing her revision in the lavatory! They insisted upon my declaiming this to them. It made a very suitable epilogue – with just the right touch of ironic banter – to what had been a very entertaining and I think mutually rewarding group.

This pleasant sense of academic and social achievement is fairly easily gained with an adult class. There is no need in adult education for the torment one feels as a teacher of adolescents in trying to appear to be both a teacher (some kind of superhuman cross between policeman, moral judge and pedagogue) and a 'real' person who suffers and enjoys all the normal human emotoins. Adult teachers lose no status and create no problems for themselves by enjoying the friendships of their classes, nor need they feel they have to act a part, conceal their ignorance and display only their strengths. Some sage and experienced adult educationists will say that they believe in behaving as if one is transparent with a class, because one is always more transparent than one realizes. These are wise words for any teacher, but they are particularly appropriate for those who teach adults.

The influence of furniture

One of the things which has given adult education its generally dusty and indifferent public image is that much of it has to take place on other people's premises, which are often intolerably ill suited to teaching adults. In the classroom itself the arrangement of the furniture and the shape of the group are extremely important, and it is here that it is often possible for teachers to have substantial influence on the atmosphere and procedures of their classes without even opening their mouths.

There are hundreds of ways in everyday life in which the way we arrange and use the furniture in a situation is a symbolic way of showing how we feel in it, or of showing what the power and communication situation is. One chair round a dining table might have arms, it is a 'carver', and in many families this chair will always be taken by the most authoritative person and will be put at what becomes the head of the table. In most churches the parson's distinctive and influential role is stressed by the fact that he stands some distance apart from his congregation, who usually sit facing him in strict rows and are not expected to make any but a unanimous response. Quakers, on the other hand, who have no priests and who encourage contributions from anyone at a meeting, arrange their chairs in a hollow square with no special places. In an office one can expect the man who leaves his desk to come and sit companionably beside his visitor to be more friendly than the man who remains firmly behind it.

Exactly the same sort of symbolic representations are at work in classrooms. A class listening to a lecture will sit in straight rows facing a lecturer, who sits or stands apart. The arrangement of the chairs emphasizes that the lecturer is a special person. In a class where a little more discussion is expected, the teacher may still stand apart, but will face students sitting in two curved rows. In a craft class where the students are working individually and expect individual attention from the teacher, they will sit at tables dotted all over the room. Where they expect to help each other and work in small groups, several desks will be pushed together. In a discussion group where the teacher is no more than chairman, the chairs might be arranged in a completely closed circle in which the teacher takes his place just like anyone else.

Desks and chairs themselves serve to emphasize roles and

relationships. It is quite usual in most classrooms to find that
the teacher's desk is larger and his chair more comfortable than
the rest of the furniture in the room. He may even be perched on
a platform – literally a 'high up'. If a teacher abandons his chair
to stand in front of his desk or perch on it, he might himself be
able to talk more informally with his students. When he is behind
his desk he is emphasizing his teacher role. In a circular or
hollow-square seating arrangement, the teacher who wants to
emphasize that he is just another member will take care to leave
his special chair alone. When he resumes his role as leader he
will return to it.

Comfortable and uncomfortable chairs, large and small groups
have other inescapable influences. Infant-sized chairs, apart from
being extremely uncomfortable, may suggest a childish role to a
student. Hard, upright chairs may communicate an unpleasantly
spartan and disciplined atmosphere. One of the most difficult
groups I have ever had in adult education was in an open prison,
where I had been asked to bring my own class to form a discussion group with some pre-release prisoners. To add to our considerable nervous uncertainty of how to conduct ourselves in so
unfamiliar a setting we had our first few meetings at one end of
an enormous cold hut, sitting in a circle on hard wooden chairs,
and generally gazing at our knees. Discussion was slow. The
improvement when we moved to a small sitting-room with easy
chairs, was amazing. No doubt this was partly because we had
by then been meeting for three weeks, but the easy chairs in
themselves seemed to suggest that we could all relax, and the
social rather than educational associations were a positive
advantage.

It does not need elaborate research (though there has been
some) to show how influential the seating is on the kinds of
communication people make and feel able to make. Clearly sheer
physical distance away from one another will tend to reduce
conversation, so that someone sitting at the back of a number of
rows is less likely to speak to the lecturer than someone at the
front. For people sitting at the front, the difficulties of twisting
round to address other people or even to see and hear other
people will generally mean that most people listen to and encourage talk from the one person who has a good view of every-

body – the lecturer. In the opposite type of group, by sitting close to people and facing them, it is extremely hard *not* to talk to them, which is why contributions to conversation in a circle are usually divided pretty evenly between members. After only a short time the pattern becomes well known to all the members and very hard to break. The longer a lecture pattern continues, the harder it is for the shyest, most silent member to speak; the longer the garrulous 'circle' group continues, the harder it is for them to listen to a lecture. In other words, the shape of the setting first influences and then reinforces the typical way in which the class behaves.

The teacher of adults who is fully aware of the range of possibilities has no need always to stick to one pattern, indeed it is most unlikely that one arrangement would suit every meeting of a dynamic class, where the different types of work being done would be reflected in different dispositions of the furniture. Thus over a term a group which started by sitting timidly in straight rows while the tutor gave basic information, explained procedures and possibilities, might then divide into small groups round separate tables for close discussion or other group work, might scatter again for individual work with reference books or work cards, might sit in a half-circle while one of the group read a paper to the others, or might revert to formal rows when it was judged a ripe time for a formal lecture from the tutor.

Changes in seating in this kind of class would occur naturally from the type of work in hand, and would not necessarily mean the restless movement this rapid description might suggest. Clearly sudden changes imposed on a group by its tutor could have disastrous effects, and could provoke this sort of rebellion:

My first group in adult education was a philosophy class held in a rural school. There were about twenty people there and I suggested we break the formal rows and sit in a circle. They did this very reluctantly but we had quite a good first meeting. The following week I arrived early and rearranged the chairs myself. I left to go and get the book box and was delayed by a conversation with the day-school head. When I returned the chairs were back in formal rows again, but the students were looking so pleased with themselves for having defied Teacher that I could not help laughing, so then they laughed and in the end we settled on a U-shape as a compromise. Arranging the chairs properly became a standing joke between us.

Obviously this class was not yet ready for the intimacy of a circular seating arrangement. They were still feeling wary of one another and of the tutor and literally wanted to keep their distance. Even in a well-established informal group, the place people choose may reflect how they are feeling about the group. As two students wrote of their own classmates:

On the first night you can always tell the people who have not been to a class since leaving school because they always sit as near the door as possible. This is in case they hate it so much that they have to make their excuses and leave.

We have one professional moaner in our group. If things do not go his way he starts getting impatient and saying in effect that he can't stand our company any longer. As the evening goes on he pushes his chair farther and farther out of the circle. If he's really feeling irritable he ends up yards away!

It is easy enough to suggest flexible seating arrangements, but to many teachers of adults this is extremely difficult. Many classes in adult education do in fact move freely and naturally from one part of a room to another during a lesson – for instance, a cookery class which watches a demonstration then returns to individual work, or a language class which uses language-laboratory booths for one part of a lesson and which then sits in a shallow circle in front of the booths for group work. But these classes occur where there is specially built accommodation. The great majority have to put up with other people's rooms, with heavy, old-fashioned wooden desks and bare floors. Sometimes the furniture is literally immovable – bolted to the floor. In such circumstances it would seem to be a better solution to ask for another room, and to hold out for it if it is not immediately forthcoming, than to endure the rigours of such furniture and the restraints it can place on the educational development of a class.

Chapter 5
The First Class

The first night of the pottery class we didn't do anything at all, we just sat there while he gave us the whole history of clay. This wasn't what I'd wanted at all. Once I'd set eyes on the clay, I wanted to get going. He just talked and talked and talked. When it came to 'question time' we were all so exhausted we couldn't think of anything to ask.

This pottery class was really marvellous. It was run by the husband of the daughter of the man I got my meat from. When I came in the tutor introduced me to the others and we got on with things straight away because we were all given a lump of clay and made thumb pots that same evening.

All the other women were about fifty or sixty and, though the course was called 'Dressmaking for Beginners', they'd all been before. They all knew each other and the tutor and they seemed to spend all their time talking about their operations. I didn't even know how to use a sewing machine but they were actually cutting out *courtelle*! The teacher told me to spend the evening looking through pattern books, so I did. It was very boring. She was supposed to be an excellent teacher – I know people went on going to her for years and years but I didn't bother to go again.

He played up the 'camp' angle if you know what I mean. Deliberately laughed at himself. But he was very frank – told us that tights were best for dancing for men and women, that men should wear jockstraps, and where we could buy all these things. We were all a bit self-conscious but he made us laugh, and even after the first ten minutes were doing a bit of dancing. It was very exhilarating.

The voluntary factor
The first class is a vitally important occasion and this is true of courses which people have to attend as for courses to which they come voluntarily. The reasons are easy to identify. The outstanding one is that if people do not like the class, they will not

bother to come again; if enough students decide not to come again the class closes, the remaining students are disappointed (and possibly angry because they have bought expensive equipment), and the teacher may lose a source of income.

Secondly, even in classes where attendance is more or less compulsory – for instance in some professional and industrial cases – first impressions are all-important. It seems as if the styles and undercurrents established in the first class, good or bad, are the ones which continue to influence students and teacher throughout the rest of the session. Adults are less indulgent than children towards a teacher. They often have a clear idea of what they want and they come to the class with a well-developed set of expectations. Furthermore, they are conscious that they are giving up their time; an adult who comes to an evening class or a day-release course is usually very much aware of the other things he could be doing instead.

The cost factor

A further factor is that adult education is not free. Even though in some areas it is still absurdly cheap for the student, in recent years adult education has felt the hardest of the pinches from the squeezes, and this situation will clearly continue for some while. Since many students are now paying much more for their classes, they are more likely to be as critical of the service they receive as they are of any other in their lives. This capacity for criticism is going to be alive and sharp at the first class, when the fee is still returnable. Even in industry, where the classes are normally free to the student, he may still be very conscious of the cost, and quick to feel that the course is a waste of money. For instance, there are management courses which cost up to £840 for an eight-week course. Few students are going to enjoy what looks like being a dismal course when they know it is costing their employers that much money.

Anxieties

Quite apart from these external standards which students apply, there are the inner worries and anxieties described earlier. In industry, where there is often some element of compulsion, people have been known to change their jobs rather than continue with a training course on which they felt they were making fools of themselves, even though by external criteria they appeared to be making good progress. Unless he absolutely has to, no one is going to continue to come to a class which constantly causes him a disagreeable amount of stress.

I was asked to attend a day-release course for shop stewards at the local tech. I wasn't too keen because it's thirty years since I was last in a classroom and I had a feeling the whole place was going to be crawling with clever dicks. I didn't think much of it from what I'd heard because we send a lot of our lads there and all they seem to do is a lot of stuff on literature and sex, watching films all day. First we had this lecture from the principal welcoming us to the college, explaining why we couldn't use the canteen, etc., then the first lesson was a long lecture on communications. It was all way above my head and I stopped listening after a bit. I knew a few other blokes there, and one of them asked a question at the end, so I suppose he'd understood all right. The chairs were very uncomfortable and I was itching to get up and stretch my legs and have a smoke. Then in the last few minutes the teacher said he wanted some volunteers to give a ten-minute talk to the rest of the class the next week. It was just like the army, no one moved, so then he suddenly turned on me and said 'Will you do that? Right, ten minutes next week.'

I couldn't have done it to save my life. When I got back to the works I made an excuse to leave the course and that was that.

Dropouts

There are several things that can be done well before the class meets to ensure that this sort of gauche and cheerless beginning to a course is avoided. Firstly, a teacher should ignore the air of hopeless resignation with which many of his colleagues regard their large dropout rate. It is true that there is some evidence to show that students often leave for reasons which have nothing to do with the quality of the course, but most of this evidence comes from efficiently administered organizations which are concerned enough about their student losses to probe the cause. All teachers ought to be concerned about absentees and leavers, and a teacher should work on the assumption that all his students in the first class are likely to go on turning up for the whole session.

A defensive line of patter, 'Of course, a lot of you will leave', is likely to become a self-fulfilling prophecy.

The prospectus

One reason for a disheartening start is that the prospectus is often too brief, or even downright misleading. A careful teacher or training officer will make sure that his course is described fully and accurately when the prospectus is being written.

Contrast these two prospectus entries for beginnners' classes in modern languages:

Mondays 7.00 p.m. Conversational French. Year 1.

Mondays 7.30–9.30 p.m. Conversational Italian for Beginners. Teacher : Mrs I. Tomassi

This is a class for people who are absolute beginners in Italian. The accent is on informality and the approach is completely conversational with the aim of helping people who wish to learn enough Italian to understand and be understood on holiday in Italy. There will be no written work but students will be asked to do some aural practice for homework. Students are asked to buy a copy of the BBC's booklet *Amici Buona Sera* (obtainable at Smith's, price 45p) and bring it with them to the first class, as some work will be based on this radio series. Other modern audio-visual aids will also be used.

The first entry tells the prospective student almost nothing, not even the name of the teacher – a surprising omission when teachers often build up impressive local reputations. It does not even give the time the class is scheduled to finish and, more important, gives no indication of the standard or the type of work required. The second entry, on the other hand, tells those interested exactly what they need to know before they sign up. Mrs Tomassi's students from last year's beginners' class can tell their friends that she is in business again; people who have no Italian are reassured that this really is a class for them; the slant of the course is firmly indicated – obviously the vocabulary will be tourist-based and this, combined with the clear emphasis on spoken skills, should be enough to deter anybody whose aim in learning Italian is to be able to read the Italian classics in the original. Students are warned to expect homework and they all know they have to buy a coursebook in advance. Not only that, enough is said about the teaching method for no one to be too surprised at the appearance of a slide projector and tape recorder in the classroom. If all goes well, Mrs Tomassi's students should already have accomplished a fair amount of work by the end of their first class.

Unfortunately the first type of entry is still quite common, perhaps because many teachers and organizers want to hedge their bets. They are afraid enrolments will go down if they are too specific in the prospectus. This seems a misplaced concern. Many more people are likely to be deterred by vague and meaningless prospectus entries than are ever put off by a precise one. There will be much less disillusion and disappointment in the first class if the teacher and his organizer have written an unequivocal and honest description of the course in the publicity material.

Enrolment

In voluntary adult education the teacher has a second chance to predict disasters before the first class. This comes at enrolment time. Some of the larger London institutes have sophisticated and well-developed enrolment procedures which amount almost to counselling. The prospective student who cannot quite make up his mind about which course to take can be interviewed by an experienced teacher and pointed in the direction of the most suitable class. Those who do know exactly what they want sign up in the usual way. Even without these processes all teachers should make every effort to be present at enrolment, as it gives student and teacher a chance to get to know one another better. The student can ask about the course and the teacher can ask the student what he wants and expects.

In industry a training officer may already know his trainees. If he does not, then there are usually opportunities for a preliminary interview before the course starts. This will give some idea of standards on both sides. In industrial training and in some other sorts of adult education the student fills in some kind of pre-course form. Although some students will regard any form filling as a tiresomely bureaucratic procedure, as indeed it can be, nevertheless a well-designed card can give the teacher the chance of a useful preview on his class, especially if the card has a space on it for special interests.

In either case, before or soon after the class starts, the teachers should also try to find out whether students have to travel a long way to reach the class and what sort of working pattern they have. Some teachers make heavy demands on students' energy without realizing that they may have had a long working day plus over-time, or a tedious bus journey. On one training scheme the mystery of why one foreman always nodded off to sleep at 5 p.m. was solved when he admitted that there was no one to take his place while he was away, so he had been getting up at 4.30 every morning to inspect the work his men had been doing the previous day.

Ideally then, the teacher comes to the first class with at least some idea of the names of the students and their likely interests. He is fairly sure that for their part they already have a clear idea of the purposes and methods of the class and have come equipped to start straight away. Where does he go from there? What should be his conduct and methods in the actual class?

Creating the right atmosphere

First, he has to remember that he must establish in two hours or so an atmosphere which would take perhaps two weeks to achieve in a school. This is why many of the outstandingly good teachers in adult education seem deliberately to aim at projecting them-selves larger than life and at persuading their students to do the same. Here, for instance, is an account of her aims in her first classes written by a strikingly successful teacher in a North Lon-don institute. She faces all the normal adult-education problems, but writ large: her classes are huge, her students, all foreigners, are of all ages, and at any one time they may contain as many as sixteen different nationalities. At the beginning the students are shy, silent and tense. The area has many Asian immigrants and there are likely to be international stresses in the class. The students are ashamed of how little English they know and it has usually taken some courage to come to the class at all.

We plunge right in on the first class meeting. My main idea is to make them laugh at me. All students can understand action jokes or facial expressions, even if they have no English, so I'm constantly acting the jokes, looking pathetic, creeping round bent up, calling myself an old lady, drawing attention to my white hair, and so on. I ask their names and perhaps if I say a few words in some of their languages – French, Spanish, Greek, Italian, Urdu – they usually understand and correct me. In this way I prove that I'm not an expert in their languages.

I always make sure we do quite a bit on the first night, but it's usually very simple things like a few prepositions – under, over, on, in, out. To teach these things I get under the table, go out of the door, stand on the chair, and while there I get the class, and then individuals, to say, 'She's under the table', 'She's on the chair'.

I always have plenty of real things to hand – bread, big jars of pickles (or sweets, so that we can all have one) – and we make up phrases about these: 'It's a bottle', 'It's a loaf', 'It's a sweet'. They are always things students will have seen in real life, but probably don't identify in English. At the end, I usually hold up an item and pretend I've got the wrong name – I always get a correct response. By the end of the class I make sure everyone has spoken at least once; usually I try to see that they've asked *and* answered a question. Quite often students who've been used to formal teaching in their own countries are very surprised at my methods. I shock some of them, I know, and they ask for books and grammar, but I concentrate on making learning enjoyable with quizzes and games. I aim to make sure everyone has a laugh during the lesson and that no one sits quietly, but that they all make great efforts to speak to me and to each other. I hope to send them out of my first class buzzing with excitement. After a couple of classes the students frequently bring friends, neighbours and other members of their family to join the class.

It is not surprising that this teacher's students make rapid progress and that the institute itself is deeply involved in the local community – for instance, running gay and highly successful 'Indian Evenings', where four or five hundred people, English and Indian, may attend to watch Indian music and dancing and to eat Indian refreshments.

The aims of this class are quite clear. The teacher has understood how nervous and suspicious the students are likely to be. She creates an atmosphere where making oneself look foolish is not only acceptable but is actually funny, and she offers herself as the first victim. Notice that although she releases tension in laughter, the class obviously does not spend all the time giggling. Plenty of work is achieved, and one of the reasons people do leave this first class exhilarated is that they do actually have something to show for it – a few phrases learnt, some English spoken, some conversation made. Not everyone can emulate this cleverly calculated clowning, but it is as well if every teacher of adults can at least show his students that he is less shy than they are.

The behaviour of the teacher in this situation has frequently been likened to those of a good host. This is a useful analogy. A good host will greet his guests, introduce them to one another, see that no one is left out. If more teachers applied these principles, there would be fewer of those occasions where the students have to wonder whether they have found the right classroom, switch the lights on themselves, or sit in uncomfortable silence because the teacher is late or can't be bothered.

The following extract shows how the 'good host' techniques are quite consciously used by a senior training officer in industry, who has a definite and well-developed method for his first classes:

First of all I greet them at the door. I say something, anything to them, like 'Have you parked?' or 'Found the room all right then?' Usually I've got some kind of background information from their companies on who they are and why they've been sent on the course, and I know all their names in theory – I'm just waiting to fit the faces to them.

I get them going on *doing* something straight away, even if it's only writing their names on a card, then I tell them a bit about myself, establishing my credentials as it were. I know they're thinking to themselves 'He's a bit of a pusher isn't he?' but I don't care. Let them think that, I know they're still curious to know what sort of a bugger they've been landed with. Then I say 'Right, now you've heard about my background – let's hear yours.' So we go round and they say 'I'm Bill Smith, I work as so-and-so's, such-and-such plant.' Usually he's so nervous he can hardly get this out without his voice wavering, so I butt in and I say 'Oh yes, Bill' (you think that's corny, but I try to get on first names straight away, none of this 'Mister' nonsense), 'you've had some trouble with the gear-cutting equipment at your place, haven't you?' He looks surprised, he's pleased, you see, and after we've had a chat about gear-cutting, he tells us a bit more about himself, and so we go on, right round the class.

Then I have another bit of spiel, I say 'I know when you walked up those steps, you thought "They're a funny looking lot, I'm not going to say anything." Everyone has that feeling, and if you don't have it, you're so lacking in modesty, you're wasting your time here.' I go on like this for a bit – it's all to get them to relax. I might spend as much as half the first class this way, I only go on to the real work when one or two of them start butting in and teasing each other, perhaps they cheek me a bit, or they all start grinning at one of my jokes instead of giving me the old stony stare. That's when I know we can get on with things, when they don't look at me as if I was a clockwork orange.

It is noticeable that both the teachers quoted are conscious of the need to get people to relax, and that they also go to some pains to make sure that everybody says something, preferably to other students as well as to the teacher. This sort of technique will emphasize to students that the accent is to be on participation and informality. Each teacher will have his own unique method of overcoming the first social shynesses of a class, but the point of this exercise is to introduce teacher to students and students to each other. By the end of the class the teacher should have learnt every student's name, and made sure that students have had a chance to learn each other's names. Learning students' names is not the great feat of memory some teachers pretend, but it is a natural courtesy. The first class is, perhaps, the only occasion where it is useful to have an attendance register actually called. Some teachers make it a policy to pause at each student's name and ask him or her a few questions, or to check on spelling, making sure that each member of the class hears the name at least twice. At later meetings of the class one of the class members could fill in the register, or else the teacher could unobtrusively mark it as each student comes in.

Sometimes even the most thoughtful and carefully made plans can fail because the atmosphere remains one of mutual shyness. This often happens when the teacher is as nervous as the students, as in this account of her first class O level English language, written by a teacher who was more used to eight-year-olds. This was her first encounter with adult education as a teacher:

The panic which I had been feeling for some time as September approached now gripped me tight. My teaching experience had all been gained in primary schools, and although I was an English graduate, I felt very out of touch with current approaches to teaching the subject. Memories of my own schooldays supplied little that seemed relevant to adults and a search through my teacher-training-course notes revealed few new ideas.

I had decided to spend the first evening in getting to know the class. My method was based on one which I had previously seen used at a weekend conference for members of a university extension course, where we had seated ourselves in a circle and the chairman had asked each one in turn to introduce himself to the group and explain why he had joined the course. In those circumstances the method had worked well; barriers were broken down and later we felt at ease with one another when discussing topics in small groups. But here it was not so successful. The bare-walled room, filled with adults cramped into apparently toy-sized desks, arranged with the stiff formality that is the mark of most classrooms at the start of the year, made everyone feel ill at ease. The fact that few of the group had ever tried to verbalize the reasons for their actions, certainly not before a mass of strangers, led to a series of ill-defined and repetitive statements uttered in barely audible tones and in a variety of accents, both British and overseas.

Inexperience and uncertainty about her role with an adult class were probably the cause of this teacher's relative failure to make a good idea work satisfactorily in practice. With this type of class, she might have done better to have adopted the technique of asking the class to write brief autobiographies, as did the redoubtable and patient Mr Parkhill, or 'Mr Pockheel', Hyman Kaplan's long-suffering teacher in the American night preparatory school for adults. Mr Parkhill appears in *The Return of Hyman Kaplan* by Leo Rosten, a book of stories which ought to be read by every teacher of adults. Mr Parkhill always asked his students at the first class to write on 'My Life'.

'Mr Parkhill felt that nothing so promptly enlisted the interest of his novitiates, so rapidly soothed their anxieties and bolstered their morale, as the invitation to recount the story of their lives.'

Fortunately, or unfortunately, not every teacher of adults has to cope with a student as boisterous and irrepressible as Hyman Kaplan, who could innocently sabotage that sort of plan with great ease.

When it came to his turn, Mr Kaplan's contribution was proudly written on the board as follows:

Hyman Kaplan
by
H*Y*M*A*N K*A*P*L*A*N

First, I was born.
In Kiev, in old contry. (Moishe Elman, famous on fiddle is also coming from Kiev.) 'Notice the sentence structure, class,' said Mr Parkhill absently; his mind was not on sentence structure at all: it was wrestling with the remorseless logic of that 'First, I was born.' *

Discussion of the course

Some teachers delay actually starting work at the first class, because they say they like to find out first what the class wants to learn. There is a delicate balance to be kept here. There is in British adult education a rather stronger tradition of student participation and of suiting the course to the needs of the student than in other sectors of the system. Sometimes this consultation with students is more lip service than anything else. Albert Mansbridge, the dedicated and determined founder of the WEA, tells a story which illustrated this point to unconsciously comic effect. He had been lecturing to a group of agricultural labourers about education. The audience was then asked what they wanted to study. There was a long silence, then one person said 'shorthand'. Mansbridge comments:

Such an answer might well have brought the proceedings to an untimely close, but somehow or other, perhaps owing to a hint from an understanding person, perhaps through a knowledge of the workings of the rural mind, which is not given to revealing its secrets or desires in public, I divined that they wished to study history.†

Yet this story is recounted by the man who in the same book can say, 'The initiative must lie with the students. They must say how, why, what or when they wish to study.'

The situation has changed now so drastically that perhaps it is

* Leo Rosten, *The Return of Hyman Kaplan*, Gollancz, 1959; Penguin, 1968.

† Albert Mansbridge, *An Adventure in Working-class Education*, Longman, 1920.

unfair to quote Mansbridge today. After all, he was writing at a time when adult education was the only academic lifeline for an intelligent working man, and it must have been hard for a clear-sighted inspiriter like Mansbridge to sit quiet while he saw potential talents frittered away in what to him were lowly aspirations. Cake, not bread, history, not shorthand, was what the WEA sought to bring to the working man.

Today we can be more certain that if people enrol for a class in a basic vocational skill then this is what they want. The reason is simply that education of all kinds, including adult education, has expanded so greatly that there is much more real choice. Certainly in urban areas, the student may have three or four institutes to choose from, and he is likely to pick a class which seems to offer something he wants, especially if the prospectus has already given him a clear idea of what to expect.

Nevertheless, there can be surprises, and it is fair that the teacher spends some of the time at the first class discussing the course with the students. There are two traps here. One is to say, helplessly, 'What would you like to do?' in tones which imply that the teacher has no more idea than the students of the subject they have enrolled to learn. The other trap, the Mansbridge one, is to ask the students what they would like to study, to listen more or less impatiently to the answers, and then to sweep them aside with, 'Oh yes, but I think what we'd better do is stick to the syllabus I've prepared.'

A sensible compromise solution would be to come to the first class with an outline syllabus already duplicated for distribution. In the light of comments made, the appropriate details can be fitted in. The advantage of coming prepared in this way is that adults enjoy seeing in advance the full scope of the subject they will be studying. Unlike children, they are not disconcerted by being reminded of the many stages that must be worked through, because they usually have a clear idea in their minds of what they want as an end product. A printed syllabus which makes it clear that there will be an end product should be a constant encouragement.

Even in industrial training, where stereotyped syllabuses and timetables are more common than in voluntary adult education, the syllabus and course should be discussed, because this is one more vital opportunity for the teacher to find out the academic levels of his group. If done clumsily this process can do more harm than good, as the following example shows:

On the first morning we all filed into the lecture room to have time-tables given out and for the 'orientation'. I didn't have a clue who the other people were, or what firms they were from, though I assumed they were all junior management like me. The first thing we did after a 'welcome' was to have a so-called discussion of the course. Straightaway Mr —, the senior lecturer, said 'Now who's got a degree here?' A few people put up their hands, just like school. I didn't and I thought, oh God, it's all going to be above my head. He spent the next thirty minutes discussing the syllabus with these people, telling them they would be learning something in spite of having degrees. Some things puzzled me about the course – for instance, I didn't know then what 'MBO' ('Management by Objectives') was, and so on. I thought, oh well, I expect I'll find out later. The only people who spoke were the degree lads and they seemed to feel very happy about the course. I didn't, but I didn't like to say so.

Concrete achievement

Whatever else is done at the first session, possibly the most important element of all is to ensure that the class members actually accomplish some of the work for which they have enrolled. However reassuring, pleasant and jolly the social atmosphere, adult students are still going to feel frustrated if they leave the class at the end of its first meeting with nothing to show for it. It is noticeable that in the descriptions of the animated and enjoyable classes quoted from students and teachers in this chapter, all of them gave the student some sense of achievement right from the beginning, whether this was a thumb pot, a few English phrases, or some dance steps learnt. What the disappointing classes share was a sense of frustration that nothing was achieved – the tantalizing clay that remained untouched, the sewing machine that could not be used. These first tasks can be very small. They should be challenging, but also carefully designed to ensure that everyone gets them right. Whatever the task, it should be of the same kind as those planned for later in the year.

Method and equipment

One of the difficulties of the teacher of adults is that many students wish to be taught in the way they were themselves taught at school. This may not be the best way to learn and it may not be the way the teacher wishes to teach. In this case it would be dishonest to dissimulate. If the teaching method really is good, let it be practised at the first class meeting and let the students see for themselves that it works. Equally, it is dishonest to pretend that homework, hard work or any other kind of student participation is not required if it is. If the teacher feels that the course will only succeed if the student does extra work at home then this must at least be discussed at the first class. 'Written work' used to be a great bogey in adult education and many thousands of anxious words were written and spoken about the necessity, difficulty and danger of wringing it out of reluctant students. This was because it was a statutory obligation on some classes and many teachers felt uneasy about signing a book to say that it had been done when in many cases it had not.

Today it is possible to be more relaxed about the subject. If a teacher feels that homework is absolutely esssential he should tell the class so, and discuss with them how it can best be achieved. For instance, a language teacher can give his class some advice on the length, kind and frequency of oral practice at home; a literature teacher can advise on how to make best use of a library system. If students say that they genuinely cannot manage to do homework, and most adults are certainly too busy to manage it in large quantities, then the teacher would be well advised to moderate the pace of the course.

Similarly, if students do not know already that they have to buy equipment, then they should be told right at the beginning what it is essential for them to buy, what is only optional, and where the equipment can be most easily and cheaply obtained. This seems a simple point, but there are classes in adult education which mope along for weeks with students who have not bothered to buy the necessary book, paintbrushes or clothing. The reason is usually that the teacher is himself half-hearted about it and manages to convey his lack of conviction to the class.

To sum up, the first time an adult class meets should be a positive and tension-releasing occasion. Teacher and students should know one another's names and something about one another's interests by the end of the first class; syllabus and methods should be discussed; and the class should actually start work as soon as possible, with a clear idea of what equipment they will need and how much homework will have to be done.

Chapter 6
Case Studies, Role Play, Simulation and Games

In a northern mining town a group of twelve miners starting a four-year day-release course grope painfully after the skills of public speaking by acting out a five-minute debate based on the national conference of their own union. It is the first time many of them have ever spoken in public. They make short, stumbling, but carefully researched speeches. This is role play, bordering on simulation. At what appears to be a completely different intellectual level, a group of new training officers several hundred miles away wrestle with problems of personnel selection by basing their discussions on a folio of documents prepared by their teacher and drawing on a real-life example. This is case study. In another setting, totally different from either of the other two, a group of trainee teachers, many of them mature students, study international relations by, over several days, dividing into four groups representing four different countries, and jockeying for prestige, economic advantage and political power, with much of the seriousness and intensity that such activities must have in the real world. This is simulation, but since each move involves points won or lost and in the final outcome one group is declared winner, it is also an example of academic gaming.

In all these groups the teacher had found a solution through stimulation and case-study techniques to the problem of how to involve adult students in the acquisition of an apparently intractable and complex mass of knowledge. The easy, neat method in every case would have been to have delivered a lecture. The rules of debate, along with one or two tricks of style, could probably be explained in two hours of lecturing; similarly the rudiments of personnel selection, or the dynamics of international relations, could no doubt have been tidily and briefly presented in lecture form. However, none of these teachers thought that it would fully meet the need of their students who, they felt, ought to experience for themselves the intricacy, excitement and perplexity of acquiring and practising knowledge. In other words, these teachers were not so much concerned with themselves and their own performances as with their students, they were not so much concerned with teaching as with learning.

There is nothing especially difficult or even novel about using simulations and case studies. Simulations will be familiar to anyone who has ever been involved in the army's military training exercises or to anyone who has seen primary-school children engaged in activities such as playing shop in the classroom. Role playing is frequently used in teaching and learning dramatic art, television documentaries have made us all familiar with the case-study approach, and academic games have their origins in games such as chess, monopoly or, much more recently, war games. In teaching adults, however, with the exception of management training, these methods of learning are used only rarely, which is a pity. The techniques are easy to apply, there is as yet no mystique and no esoteric jargon. One of the few difficulties is the purely academic one of nomenclature. People tend to use the same names to describe different situations; definitions are only rarely attempted. This is understandable enough, as in practice each one contains elements of the other, and it may be impossible to distinguish case studies from role playing, or role playing from simulation and simulation from academic gaming, because there is a point at which each one blends into the next.

The simplest way of understanding these four techniques is to look at them as four increasingly elaborate and participatory versions of the same basic art – a way of learning general principles through being involved in a particular situation, usually one which could occur in real life, but with some of the real-life time intervals and distracting detail smoothed out for purposes of laying bare the essentials.

Case studies can be prepared through folders of documents, collections of descriptive material, tapes, television or film, or mixtures of all these, and would be presented to a group simply as the basis of discussion. Role playing might take the process a stage further, when members of the group acted out and improvised roles and situations using the information they obtained from the case-study material. This might become a full-scale simulation if it was carried out continuously and intensively over several hours using fairly elaborate printed, filmed or recorded material, with fresh problems and complications introduced from time to time by the lecturer. It becomes an academic game if it is conducted by competing teams or individuals, who are awarded points on the basis of moves and decisions they make in relation to one another.

Definitions are, of course, never satisfactory descriptions of what actually happens in the classroom, and in practice I have seen case studies more intensive, protracted and elaborately documented than many simulations, just as I have seen role playing that was little more than a bit of drama improvised off the cuff by teacher and students alike, and academic games that had virtually lost their right to be called means of learning at all, since they had become stereotypes rituals played for their own sakes, with the gaming element predominating.

Use and method in the classroom

How is this type of classroom exercise organized and carried out? Some role playing is so simple that it hardly needs any preparation at all and is absorbed without fuss into work already being done. For instance, in a discussion for shop stewards on running branch meetings, it would be perfectly natural for a teacher to suggest that instead of simply talking about different kinds of chairmanship, the students might actually try them. In language teaching, role playing may seem a normal extension of work done practising dialogues and drills, and only becomes more recognizably something novel and different when the teachers sets up a 'scene' with the appropriate props. For instance, in one French conversation class the teacher bases the first part of the class time on an episode from a radio language series where the characters are ordering food in a restaurant. The students sit in their normal places while they are repeating the dialogue and drills, but they then move in groups of four to a table in one corner of the room which is perfectly laid out for a meal. The tablecloth, wine, knives and forks, butter, mustard, menu, bread, bread basket and, finally, money are all French. The students 'play' the characters in the series, but extend the dialogue according to improvisations of their own and in response to the teacher, who sometimes plays waiter, sometimes another diner. After corrections and discussion they then play the same scene again.

There is no one ideal way of preparing and carrying out role play and simulation. Some teachers prefer to involve the group in researching the case-study material themselves: preparing speeches for a debate or preparing cases for negotiations in an industrial agreement is one way of doing this. In this case the teacher simply presents the group with the barest outlines of the situation a week or a few days beforehand. Other teachers favour variations on what is known in management training as the 'in-basket exercise', where the group members are presented with a batch of case-study material – letters, records, memos, press reports – such as might appear in an in-tray, and are required as individuals and under considerable time pressure to reach the kind of decisions they may need to make in real life.

More usually the teacher will involve the whole class in group activity, either all together, in small groups, or in small groups which watch each other and then discuss. Sometimes he will give the whole group all the information available, sometimes he will deliberately hold back certain crucial pieces of information and will wait for the group to ask for it, sometimes he will supply a group or an individual with background information or documents not available to the others.

The form in which the brief is given will also vary. Simple presentation is usually best and always cheapest. Using a battery of media for their own sakes – closed-circuit television, tape, film, overhead projectors – can be confusing, and sometimes has the effect of making students feel they are acting out a private fantasy for the teacher.

Whatever the form, the general pattern would be something like this:

1. The teacher decides what skill he is trying to teach, how many hours of class time he can devote to the exercise, how many participants can be involved.

2. He, or the group, prepares case-study material and the group is briefed on exactly what problem or skill they are exploring and why. It is most important to alert the group in advance, otherwise role play can be a waste of time. Case-study material is distributed.

3. Students are given a set period of time to prepare their case

and are told how much time there will be altogether. At this stage they can decide what the rules, if any, are to be.

4. The students then act out the situation, improvising what they think would be the behaviour of the people in the case.

5. The most important part of the whole exercise is the follow-up discussion, because it is at this point that insights can be sharpened, solutions compared and learning consolidated. Important questions for teacher and students to ask might be: How did the participants behave – were they thoughtful, tactful, overbearing, aggressive? Did they look for underlying reasons for behaviour, or were they satisfied with superficial ones? Could the decisions made be justified? What administrative machinery would be needed to carry them out? Why were certain decisions taken or not taken? What frustrations and irritations did the participants feel? Is this how people feel in the parallel real-life situations? How would one set about finding more information which might have a bearing on the case? What basic skills are involved in the situation?

Two examples will show the sort of material that can be used. In the first, a very simple case study, a group of foremen at the beginning of a day-release course were tackling role play for the first time.

Dealing with subordinates

Late without leave

Aim of this case study. To look at problems arising out of questions of discipline and relationships with subordinates.
Time available. One and a half hours.
Method. The class should divide into three groups of five. There will be thirty minutes for discussing the case and trying to arrive at a solution.

The groups reconvene, and each group will role play its solution to the others. The tutor will play the role of John Pickles and can be asked for further information during the pre-role-play session.

The final three-quarters of an hour will be spent in discussing the various solutions and in exploring the supervisory problems arising out of this sort of issue.
Background information. Butchards, a medium-sized engineering firm, have recently recovered from two serious disputes over pay and

working conditions. The men in the 'black' machine shop had complained that their 'black money' for particularly unpleasant work was not high enough. 'Black money' was increased as a result of the strikes, but only to about half the amount asked by the union. Management have said that the order book was too slim to bear a greater increase. Since the disputes they have been making a concerted drive to reduce absenteeism and lateness. After recent negotiation with the shop stewards all employees have received notices in their pay packets to the effect that persistent lateness without good reason will be followed by dismissal. The shop stewards are uneasy about the agreement and are looking for a test case which they hope they can also use as a lever to reopen the 'black money' negotiations. The works manager has promised that there will always be proper investigation of every case. He avows that victimization is *not* what management wants.

Characters and situation. Bob Painter is twenty-four, a semi-skilled fitter in the 'black' machine shop. Well known as a live-wire, enjoys practical jokes, prone to making provocative statements about Chairman Mao and workers' control in China. Bright, intelligent, can be every foreman's *bête-noire*. Never actually puts a foot wrong, has excellent production record. His first serious mistake ever is to be a regular three-quarters of an hour late three mornings running. He offers no excuse, doesn't speak to anyone, goes straight to his work, ignoring whistles and jokes from the other men.

Harry Fletcher is thirty-three; has only just been appointed foreman in this section, traditionally the toughest in the factory. He takes his job seriously and has been given strict instructions by management to enforce the new rule on lateness. He sees Painter arrive late, tells him he's had his last chance, and sacks him on the spot. Painter leaves without a word.

By midday John Pickles, aged forty-two, experienced senior shop steward, has brought the men out in his section. Their stoppage can halt the whole factory within twenty-four hours. He says the men will not go back to work until Painter is reinstated.

What does Fletcher do?

In this exercise the part of the shop steward was played by the teacher. He is the only one who 'knows' that Bob Painter's wife is in hospital with a threatened miscarriage and that he has been made late because he has had to get his five-year-old daughter off to school himself. He does not reveal this information unless absolutely obliged to. The roles are played successively by three different groups of students and then analysed by the whole group. Each 'scene' lasts only five minutes, but the whole exercise takes an hour and a half of class time because there is detailed discussion of company rules, of procedure for avoiding disputes in the engineering industry, of union rules, and of the human problems created by being charged with responsibility for discipline in industrial situations.

The second example is taken from a full-scale simulation designed to suit a three-hour session planned for a group of parents on 'Education Today'. The simulation centred on a case study (details disguised but taken from a real-life case) of an eleven-year-old whose parents were faced with the tricky problem of wanting their child to go to a different school from the one in which he was offered a place by the education authority. The aims of the simulation were: to inform parents about the current system in their area, to explain their rights within it, to explore some of the personal stresses involved in parent–school relationships, to discuss the criteria on which choice of school might be based.

The documents themselves would be too lengthy to reproduce here but they included:
1. The child's last primary-school report.
2. A medical report.
3. Two essays written by the child on 'My Ideal School' and 'My Family'.
4. Confidential report on the child from the primary-school head to the chief education officer.
5. Copies of correspondence between parents, heads and the chief education officer.
6. Long extracts from the two secondary-school prospectuses.
7. Extracts from the 1944 Education Act.
8. Extracts from the 1960 'Manual of Guidance' for parents.

Advantages

When done well, what are the advantages of this type of learning? Firstly, and probably the most important for adults, the element of realism makes it an eminently suitable way for them to learn. Adults are usually impatient of teaching which seems remote from the realities of whichever skill they are learning; they want to feel that no time is wasted on vague theory which is going to be of little real relevance and practical value to them. Thus, if a course for shop stewards is called 'Industrial Relations' the course members may not take at all kindly to lectures on economic theory or historical development of trade unions, however vital the lecturer might feel this information is to understanding current conflicts. Members of such courses are inclined to say that since they conduct their real-life negotiations in an atmosphere of hustling, keen controversy, they expect to see the same atmosphere understood and catered for on the course. It is even better if the same realistic conditions can enter the process of learning itself, only in a way that more information can be fed in, in conditions of more certain control than is usual in real life, where inflamed or tender feelings often mean a stubborn refusal to accept new information at all. The realistic atmosphere in simulation is achieved through the careful preparation of the stimulus material, and also by the fact that students take roles where they start behaving as people might in a wider variety of situations than is usual in the classroom.

Simulation can also bring an element of realism and excitement to academic subjects by inviting decisions in a re-created historical, geographical or sociological situation. Thus students of history who might be studying the battle of Waterloo could be given maps of the battle ground, pins to represent groups of soldiers in the different armies, letters, memoranda, biographies and so on, and could play out for themselves the crucial moves of the battle. In teaching geography to children some successful games have been developed round events such as the building of the great North American railways, where children have in fact learnt the geography of the country, the map of the routes, and the reasons railways were built when and where they were through the use of a geography game. No doubt simulations could be developed along the same lines for adults.

A second important advantage of role playing and simulation is that they are entirely active methods of learning. Earlier chapters have attempted to show how important activity is to adult learning, and have stressed how adults need not just to be told how to do something, but instead to try it out for themselves. Indeed, simulation may offer a unique chance in certain subjects to bridge the yawning gap between theory and practice. This can be one of the most unyielding problems of planning a piece of teaching where, as in management, shop-steward education or teacher training, students will frequently complain that the theory they learnt was a hopelessly inadequate preparation for facing the real situation. Some kind of simulation or role play may be the only possible way trade unionists and managers can learn the art of thinking quickly under pressure, or the only way that one can learn how to conduct an interview or chair a meeting.

A further advantage of simulation and role play here is that because it is a realistic, active method, it has many of the features of learning in real life, with the powerful difference that in real life mistakes made can be expensive, disagreeable and mortifying. In role play mistakes can be made without retribution. The atmosphere of calm analysis and good-humoured support from tutor and other students makes it possible to see why mistakes have been made and to learn to avoid them in future. In this way a student, who in a business game makes a gross error which in real life would have cost him his job, can step back and analyse what moves led him (or the character he was playing) to act as he did. An added convenience is that because of its telescoped time-scale, simulation can present the student with situations he is unlikely to encounter every day, and might indeed wish to avoid, but which nevertheless he ought to be prepared to meet. Thus role play and simulation in a public-speaking class might introduce a particularly odious heckler character; an industrial-relations course for shop stewards might include a difficult situation both with management and with another union.

In a full-scale simulation this telescoped time-scale has the further advantage that it makes it possible to see the effect of one's decisions and actions in a rapid way that is not normally possible in the real situation – in other words, there is almost instant 'knowledge of results'.

Because role playing usually arouses powerful emotions in those who take part, it can be a potent and valuable method to any teacher whose subject involves the development of sensitivity and tolerance. Crude attitude-change is not generally held to be a desirable educational aim in adult education, but increasing understanding in a way that may lead to attitude change certainly is. In subjects such as politics, sociology, industrial relations, religion or literature, many issues can only be approached through a genuine understanding not just of one other point of view, but of the possibility that a whole range of viewpoints may be equally valid. Thus shop stewards, often reluctantly persuaded at first to prepare a set of management as well as union cases for a piece of role playing, may come to understand the strengths and weaknesses, the varying opinions at different levels of seniority, of both management and union situations in a way that would be impossible from a more passive, intelectualized analysis. Where 'role reversal' is used and after the first run through the participants play each other's roles, this effect is particularly noticeable.

Even more intangible benefits of this kind of role playing and simulation is that their real value may be in the 'social skills' they teach. Supporters of this point of view would say that what is important on many courses is not absorbing the content of any particular mass of information so much as learning to understand how one's own behaviour appears to other people, to work in a group and to solve a problem, to accept other people's solutions, their contributions and their right to disagree.

Specific aims

Most people enjoy role playing and simulation, perhaps largely because of its rousing effect on the emotions. But the benefits are far from being confined to the emotional delights of acting out and creating conflict, discussion and debate. Role playing and simulation can be designed specifically to meet some of the fundamentally serious aims of any course – to teach people how to acquire, evaluate and use information. Thus in the miner's day-release class, the second of the debating exercises was a motion on whether or not 'social wages' ought to be increased. Chairman, proposers, opposers, seconders, and speakers from the floor had all been asked to prepare their material over the fortnight between class meetings. The speeches revealed that the students had been driven for their sources to Blue Books, to books on social policy, to newspaper libraries and to their own remembered experience. This information had to be collated and assessed for what it was worth and presented cogently to the rest of the class. This was a class in preliminary education, the class members men whose formal education, such as it was, had been unsatisfactory, and who had barely even written a letter or read a book for perhaps fifteen years. Yet their speeches, brief, stumbling and stiff though they were, showed how the processes of active search, assessment and presentation of information had already begun. Even more so, in the burst of relieved and flowing discussion that followed the tension of formal debate it was possible to see how fact, opinion and rumour were beginning to be weighed with shrewdness and insight: 'How do you *know* that people come from abroad just to get our welfare benefits? Who says?' and, 'It's too sweeping to say our benefits are good. There are firms in France and Germany who *give* more away than the State does here.'

On a much more elaborate scale another group, who had enrolled for a course in urban planning, undertook a simulation which was worked in pairs over two intensive three-hour sessions separated by a week. To work out several possible solutions to a single problem in traffic control and urban redevelopment, the group were obliged to look up, absorb and use some or all of: Town and Country Planning Acts, several classic studies in urban sociology, local history, academic analyses and appreciations of Georgian architecture, and some elementary principles of civil engineering. During the course of the simulation the teacher presented them with additional complications in the form of resolutions passed by local pressure groups, or announcements of new findings on sites of historical value. Here the group was involved in a highly sophisticated and elaborate project involving research skills, information retrieval and problem solving, as well as learning to weigh social priorities and to argue and present a case in the final report. The students' own opinion of the exercise was, devastatingly, that they had learnt more in the two simulation classes and in the following class devoted to discussion and analysis than they had learnt in all the rest of the course put together.

Student's involvement

There does not seem any doubt that simulation and role playing generates intense involvement among those taking part and that it is an excellent way of motivating people who might find it difficult to learn in other ways. It is almost impossible to remain aloof and uninvolved. Even the most stately student usually finds it hard to stay outside. Most students start by thinking it is going to be a laugh, something they will go along with to humour the teacher. They then rapidly pass to the stage where they are involved but keep some superficial sense of joking, distance or irony. In a class such as the urban-planning group where the basic emphasis is on academic skills this often remains the predominant mood. Where the whole group is also involved in role playing, even this mood passes, replaced by an entirely absorbed seriousness for the task in hand.

Mixed abilities

One of the problems which teachers of adults tend to find most vexing is the mixed abilities of their classes. In despair at the difficulties of ever coping with what often seem impenetrable tangles of age, intelligence and educational experience, some teachers will even start talking in heretical terms of 'streaming' or 'creaming'. Simulation and role playing is immensely adaptable for classes of mixed ability. It offers natural opportunities for working in groups, for occasions where students of different abilities can help each other, and where distinctions between bright and not so bright can at least be blurred if not extinguished altogether.

The teacher's role

Many teachers are also bothered by the apparent inevitability of their own dominant role in the classroom. Simulation, like the discovery method or project work, involves a fundamental change in the teacher's role. He is still very much in the centre of things since he prepares at least the initial materials, and in the class itself he will usually retain a central and coordinating position. Neverthelss, his most hectic work is done before the class meets, and his traditional role of giving information to all his students simultaneously is certainly eroded. The emphasis shifts to the resources used, to the students themselves, and to the creative contributions they are able to make with the teacher's encouragement. In this way, too, the 'problem' of student participation melts away. Students participate as a matter of course because activity is built into the whole exercise.

Problems of resources

Every novelty in educational method brings with it some danger that devotees will recommend it as a cure-all for every classroom malaise. It is unlikely that any one method will be right for every class all the time, and this is as true of simulation, case studies and role play as of any other method. Role playing and simulation are not all plain sailing for teacher or learner. Although they are highly flexible methods and once prepared can be used with a variety of different classes, the preparation can be lengthy and exacting. Furthermore, the need for stylish presentation and for individual student copies means that expense may rule out simulation as a method for the part-time teacher in the sort of evening institute which has only limited finances, where there is only a part-time secretary, and duplicating facilities are either non-existent or strictly rationed.

For teachers working in institutions with good audio-visual aid resources, the situation is much easier. Tapes, slides, printing and duplicating can be ordered and without any of the above-the-line trouble and persuasive talk that may be involved in buying a set of books. Some commercially produced simulations do exist, but these are usually only available from the United States and are noticeably American in style and interest.

More promising sources of case-study material on which simulations and role playing could be built and extended by the individual teacher are now being increasingly promised by publishers and broadcasters. The Jackdaw series (folders with facsimile documents, letters, diary entries, charts) on history topics such as the abolition of slavery or the history of trade unions make excellent material for historical simulation. In broadcasting there have been recent series where broadcasting authorities have deliberately aimed to supply adult groups with filmed, recorded and printed case-study material. One example was a television series for teachers, where a series of fairly straightforward programmes on curriculum development and management in schools was accompanied by an excellent publication prepared by William Taylor. This spiral-bound book contained chapters of plain exposition interleaved with several coloured pages of case-study material based on a fictional school.*

The BBC has also been increasingly providing material of this sort. Many educational series on industrial relations have been built around the case-study/documentary idea, sometimes with supporting publications. For instance the 1968 radio series 'Case Studies in Industry' was accompanied by a folder containing loose sets of documents to go with the 'case' for each programme. Usually the fact that the printed material is designed so that it can be independent of the programmes themselves gives an added flexibility to the possibilities for use by teachers.

Emotional display

Teachers who have not used role playing and simulation tend to brood anxiously about the potential dangers of inviting too much emotional involvement from students. Adult classrooms generally tend to be peaceful places and many teachers rightly hesitate before plunging their students into what might turn out to be an embarrassing emotional display.

It is for this reason, no doubt, that of the four techniques described in this chapter, case study is by far the most commonly used, precisely because it allows emotional issues germane to the group to be discussed coolly at a distance in terms of other people's problems, but without any of the apparent hazards involved in role playing. It is true that in role playing some students may be alarmed by the passionate response a role-play situation draws from them, or from others. It is true that some role playing becomes nearly indistinguishable from the real thing. But in practice it is never *quite* the real thing, tempers never run quite so high, one's emotions are never quite so fully engaged as they are in the real situation, because however realistic the setting, the problem or the incidental detail, one never forgets that one is in a learning situation. Particularly where the teacher has stressed that it is not their own but other people's roles that students are to play, there is always some sense of distance between action and thought. In a group which has become experienced in using the technique, there is a noticeable feeling that it is quite all right to

*William Taylor, *Heading for Change*, Harlech Television, 1969.

indulge the emotions a situation may provoke because these emotions are in themselves valuable source material for the follow-up discussion and analysis.

Student anxieties

A more real difficulty, especially at first, is the opposite one that adult students may refuse to become involved at all, they may not wish to step out of the conventionally passive student role into something that seems to bear a suspicious resemblance to amateur dramatics. A student who is nervous about speaking in public may be even more embarrassed about role playing. This difficulty arises most often where role playing is used in academic subjects, when it will be most noticeably in conflict with traditional methods of teaching and where it probably grows less naturally and genuinely out of the work than out of subjects where the basic art being taught is skill in human relationships. A student who has enrolled for what looks like being a straightforward enough course in international relations may well feel as peeved about the introduction of academic gaming as the man who finds that his comfortable, undemanding local pub has gone in for poetry readings. If role playing and simulation can only be introduced with a great fanfare and with much special pleading from the tutor, then it is probably unsuited to the course. In any case it is probably best tried gradually without fuss and on a small scale at first.

Problems for the teacher

One of the reasons students may be suspicious of role playing and simulation is that it is not an orderly, predictable method of learning. There are no prepackaged maxims that can be transferred direct from teacher to learner. On the contrary, the student not only has to elaborate on a given situation by actively interpreting it, he then has to deduce the general rules for himself. This is why the follow-up discussion is so important. It is also why learning through simulation, role playing and case study takes so much longer and is so much more diffuse and sprawling than a series of lectures. Use of these techniques therefore makes considerable demands on the teacher, not only in the time and skill they will demand in preparation, but also in his ability to train his groups to generalize a clear overall picture from a series of specific examples.

It is perhaps the most common failing of teachers of groups using simple case-study material that they are often unable to encourage the group to look beyond the rights and wrongs of a particular case. If the material intrigues the group they will sometimes argue it endlessly, but take it no farther than that. If the material is less absorbing the group may tend to discuss it in a desultory way for a short time, but will then dismiss it by implying that because conditions in their factory, school or locality are not exactly like the ones in the case study, there is nothing to be learnt from it. This is a particularly pressing problem with industrial workers, who will often have a narrow but extremely intensive practical knowledge of their own cases while rejecting the applicability of either general theory or other cases to their own.

A first necessary step might be to demonstrate through role play that even their own case looks different when seen from different angles, but progress here is bound to be slow. With such groups case study, role play and simulation done badly is particularly frustrating for the students, who are understandably inclined in such circumstances to start muttering in favour of bringing back formal methods where at least the outward trappings of learning – talk and chalk, headings and subheadings – are familiar.

Another real enough shortcoming, particularly of case-study techniques, is that there is never as much information available as there would be in real life. Students will often criticize a slackly prepared case study on these groups by saying that they cannot possibly argue the case without more information. I once sat in with a group of senior managers who were being invited to solve a problem based on a difficult business situation. Discussion was slow because the case study itself had been too crudely drawn. In the end the group decided that the only way their discussion could be turned into something useful to themselves was for them to decide what *extra* information they would have needed in order to solve the problem. In real life there are, of course, often severe limitations on the amount of information that is available. Most teachers believe that case studies must and should omit confusing and conflicting detail, though some exponents of case-study and simulation techniques would stress that it is sometimes necessary to introduce this too, to teach relevance and choice. But in general there must be simplification, not so much that the case is hopelessly falsified to the state where students will reject it, never so complicated that it is beyond the current capacities of the group to solve. Where the case study is extended into role play some of this danger recedes because the case itself takes on the added dimensions which live participants must give.

More serious criticisms can be made of academic games than of any of the other methods discussed in this chapter. Their competitive element probably makes them unsuitable for teaching adults, and the very word 'game' may suggest that the activity is childish or not to be taken seriously, though their supporters would say that business games are uniquely valuable in teaching decision making and strategy. But games tend to be inflexible; most of those on the market are obtainable only with difficulty; like published case studies they are mostly American in origin. The teacher's attempts to devise home-made games may land him in a tropical growth of rules and points which are eventually rejected by the group as artificial.

Research findings

As yet there is only meagre evidence from research about whether case study, role playing, simulation and gaming are effective methods of learning. Some studies have been made, but these largely concern management training, or with work schoolchildren; in any case, they suggest few general rules for teachers of adults. Role playing, it seems, does improve social sensitivity, particularly where sharp, crisp analysis and discussion follows it. If there is no follow-up, students may simply become better at role playing without learning any general skills. Case studies may stimulate discussion, but some teachers report a tendency to find wild solutions generated by precisely that sense of unreality which the case study is designed to avoid. Simulation seems to arouse intense motivation and involvement in academic and non-academic children alike; it may well have the same reliable effect with adults, but it is too early to say with any certainty. In any case even in the research that has been done, the results clearly depend on the excellence of the material used and on the professional skill and personality of the teacher. For instance, some of the disappointing results of inquiry into case-study methods may be due to the poor quality of the material and on the teacher's uncertainty in handling it.

Reliable research into teaching method is notoriously difficult to design, perhaps particularly so in this area where a wide range of teaching possibilities can shelter under one roof. In the meantime there is plenty of empirical evidence from enthusiasts that suggesting strongly that the methods do work when planned with care and thought, and when used not blanket-fashion, but in judicious combination with other forms of learning.

Pat Tansey and Derek Unwin, whose book on simulation is the only general survey of the subject, commented:

What can we claim for simulation at the moment? Merely that it is an *alternative* method of instruction. Not a *better* method, but we must get out of the habit of measuring in the comparative sense. It is essential to recognize that if there is a job to be done, and the job has any worth or significance, then there are alternative ways to do the job. It must be acknowledged that most training methods have some unique advantages and that while it is possible to decide that under one set of variables a single method is best, that method may be impracticable under a different set of circumstances. If a person or a group cannot learn using one method, then it is as well to have an alternative way of teaching a process. This is the function of simulation.*

* P. J. Tansey and Derek Unwin, *Simulation and Gaming in Education*, Methuen, 1969.

Chapter 7
Discovery Learning and Programmed Instruction

I hear and I forget
I see and I remember
I do and I understand
OLD CHINESE PROVERB

The teacher's time

There is a story in adult education of the visitor to a dress-making class who was baffled by the large cards he noticed propped on every student's table. Each card had a different label. One said 7.15, another 7.21, another 7.42 and so on. When he inquired what the cards signified he was told, 'Oh, that's when Mrs — comes round to give us our individual teaching.'

This true story seems to me sad because it is about a class where the teacher had assumed that the only way her students could learn was by one-to-one demonstration and practice. Since she had a lot of students, she had carefully divided the time available by the number of students and had also come up with what no doubt seemed an ingenious way of parcelling out her time and of reassuring her students that they really could expect individual help. History does not relate what the students were expected to do during the rest of the class time.

All teachers, and not only teachers of skills, face the same problem this teacher faced: twenty or so students cannot all be overseen at once, yet individual instruction of some kind may be what they need and expect. Indeed, in some craft classes in adult education the expectation of individual tuition may be so powerful that what starts out as a promisingly congenial atmosphere is spoiled by jealous suspicions that the teacher is spending a few minutes more with one student than another.

In many cases such suspicions are bound to be justified. In the normal two-hour class with twenty students, if there are a few minutes for a coffee break, a few more for a demonstration or for setting up equipment, if each student were to receive an equal amount of the teacher's time this would only come to about four and a half minutes each. Clearly this is far too brief. The bold students store up their queries and have them sorted out in one rush, the shy ones say little; for most students neither bold nor shy, their exclusive time with the teacher is too short for much more than the teacher's cursory inspection and general encouragement, which is why most teachers tend to stay longer with each student in the hope of distributing their favours more fairly next time the class meets.

In other ways, too, this is an unsatisfactory situation. The normal pattern of craft classes, or indeed of classes in science and mathematics, is that they start with or include a demonstration by the teacher. It is because demonstration alone is such an unsatisfactory method of learning for adults that the student comes to place so much value on individual attention from the teacher. A demonstration tends to flash past swiftly in the student's mind; in trying to memorize its various stages the adult student is forced to rely on short-term memory and on a speedy pace of understanding, in both of which, as research has shown (see chapter 2), he is at a disadvantage. One of the typical features of a skilled performance is how absolutely rapid and effortless it looks. Even when deliberately slowed down, the movements performed by a craftsman will be beautifully fluid and economical, but fairly useless to the onlooking learner. Indeed, the sole value of demonstration may be that it shows what a skilled performance *looks* like – profitable when the student has nearly acquired the skill satisfactorily, confusing to a beginner.

In general the answer to these difficulties is to bring about a situation where the teacher is no longer the only source of information and expertise, where the number of resources is increased and along with them the amount of work the students can do unaided.

In the dressmaking class described below the teacher revolutionized her class with little fuss by increasing the number and sharpening the quality of the simple home-made resources available and moving them into the centre of the educational stage. From being mere 'aids' they became the means of instruction, a way of presenting a series of taxing problems through which her unusually mixed class learned.

I started my method several years ago when I had a dressmaking class where complete beginners and advanced students were all mixed up together. It was impossible to find one topic to suit everybody. I felt I wanted to give most time to the beginners, but there was also a need to persuade the advanced people to be more adventurous.

I began by preparing handwritten duplicated sheets of instructions and drawings to go with sets of small pieces of fabric already cut out from my own scrap box. I seem to remember that this first exercise was a quite difficult one on pin tucking and seaming, a topic several students had been querying but had been too timid to attempt. I suggested that each week we might spend half an hour on a similar project, then the rest of the time they could continue their own work. I explained that everything they needed to know to produce perfect work was contained on the sheet and that they had no need of me for explanations except in emergencies.

There were some long faces at first but the method seemed to succeed more or less straight away. Since each member of the group had a different fabric they naturally achieved different effects which caused a lot of useful discussion in which the students learned from each other. (I make a point of encouraging informal discussion. I always join them for this as I feel it is here that the class is really learning.)

More and more time was taken up on the 'experimental' work. It eventually spread out over the next year to designing their own clothes. The confidence given by learning *on their own* to master some of the most intricate techniques in dressmaking spread to the clothes they made for themselves and their children, which were creditably adventurous in design and execution.

The beginners began to feel left out so I was soon using the method with everybody. The duplicated sheets needed alteration – some proved too detailed, others too scanty – and were also too flimsy for constant use. The next lot were nicely typed and mounted on plastic card. At one stage I was nearly put back in the old situation. So much excitement, so many queries came that I almost could not cope. I started filing the work sheets in expanding document cases, compiling loose-leaf folders of reference material, card indexes and later on colour slides to which the class themselves constantly contributed and referred and to which they were directed by each week's work cards. Advanced students helped prepare material for beginners and one gradually builds up a stock of first-class material. My own store of fabric would have run out quickly if the principal had not had the idea of writing to textile factories for scrap.

My suitcase quickly got far too heavy to carry round everywhere, particularly when I started to feel we always needed the slide projector handy. Fortunately that problem, too, was solved when the day-school home crafts teacher became interested in the method and offered us the use of a large cupboard for storage.

The approach this teacher used and the way she developed it – informal, exploratory and free ranging – seems to have been arrived at without reference to any particular theory of learning, but it is in fact close in spirit to many modern methods of learning. The teacher's materials, carefully prepared beforehand, amended and improved after trial with the class, freed her to take a less restricted, more consultative role in the classroom. All the students were able to work unaided in small groups or as individuals and to be fully involved in a challenging carefully planned kind of learning for the full two-hour stretch. This is a very different situation from that in the conventional dressmaking class, where the amount of new learning each week is probably quite small: the students are dependant on the teacher's personal attention and spend a lot of time doing the sort of simple sewing they could as easily do at home.

Many recent trends in educational theory and practice have reinforced the idea that new materials, methods and resources must be prepared so that a lesson becomes more certainly an occasion when teaching suits the learner. Where the teacher is constantly on his hind legs lecturing or demonstrating, particularly in adult education with its often uneasy mixtures of age and ability, his lesson can become like so much grapeshot, some of it hitting the target, much of it flying wide. Among the more promising of a cluster of ways of resolving the situation are two closely allied methods – discovery learning and programmed instruction.

Discovery learning

'Learning by discovery' and 'learning by doing' are phrases mostly misapplied and misunderstood in education. Discovery learning should not mean that the student muddles about till by some happy chance he hits on the right answer. This is trial-and-error learning and is rightly condemned by most teachers as frustrating and time wasting. It is true that in primary education discovery learning still strongly values the spontaneity in learning provoked by children's interests, but even in the primary school, when thoughtfully carried out, discovery methods are a structured way of learning. The task to be learned has been carefully analysed and the learner has been presented with or has found enough information for him to form the conclusions himself. Discovery methods in schools are associated now with the new materials and methods suggested by the work of the Nuffield Foundation and the Schools Council in mathematics and science. In industrial training it is associated with the work of Eunice Belbin and Meredith Belbin.*

Experimental findings

The Belbins' work in developing their own precisely defined methods of training is probably of most significance to the teacher of skills and simple theoretical background in adult education or in industry, as it is a method specially developed for older learners and has proved efficient and reliable in a whole series of experiments.

An example will show something of the method and its scope. One of Dr Meredith Belbin's projects was to help re-train British Rail steam-locomotive engine drivers so that they were capable of driving diesel electric trains. The work with the first men, where they trained on an elaborate simulator with rocking driving cabs and projected film, showed that there was not too much difficulty with straightforward driving. The two types of train were sufficiently alike to make it fairly easy to transfer the skills of driving a steam train to those necessary to drive a diesel. Where the men did find difficulty was in understanding the theoretical and technological aspects of the new trains. It was vital that they should have such understanding as if, for instance, a circuit fails on a train, the driver must be able to locate it quickly and take the right action himself, otherwise not only his train but many others might be delayed.

The discovery method was used to teach basic principles of

*E. Belbin, 'Training the adult worker', 1964; R. M. Belbin, 'The discovery method in training', *Training Information Paper*, no. 5, HMSO, 1969.

electricity to men who mostly had only the vaguest theoretical knowledge of the subject. The trainees worked in pairs with three progressively more complicated sets of wooden boards. The first board carried a battery, an ammeter and a switch. Each pair was also given a bulb, a bulb holder, a more powerful battery, two small electric motors, and some wire and clips. Written instructions told them which pieces of apparatus to assemble with which, invited them to take away, add and experiment in various ways with the apparatus on the boards, then to observe and draw conclusions.

This was the first part of the instruction sheet:

Instructions for use of equipment

1. Look at the electrical circuit laid out on the board. It contains a battery, a bulb, a switch and an ammeter. Make sure you can see each of these things.
Starting at one side of the battery, the wire goes to the ammeter. It then goes to the —, then to the —, and then back to the —. Where does the needle point on the ammeter? —.
Press the switch down.
The ammeter needle now shows — amps.
The bulb —.
Now unclip the wire from one side of the battery and press the switch.
The ammeter needle now shows — amps.
The bulb —.
Clip the wire back on the battery and press the switch again.
Does the bulb light now? —. What does the ammeter show? —.
Now unclip the wire from the bulb and press the switch. What does the ammeter show? —.
Does the bulb light? —.
The current flows only if the switch is — and all the wires are —.
The circuit can be broken by unclipping a wire or by the —.
Switches are an easy way for us to break a — when we wish. But wires are usually — by accident. Either way, if the circuit is broken — happens.

In this way, instead of listening passively to an instructor who told them how a circuit works, or who drew it for them on the blackboard, the trainees actually constructed a circuit themselves, they saw through their own observed experience that electrical circuit must have an undisturbed path before it can flow from one pole of the battery to another. Instead of struggling with verbal explanations of a new word like 'ammeter', they saw for themselves and made use of the fact that it measured the flow of current. From these simple beginnings the trainees worked through this and two more boards, the last of which simulated the power circuit of a diesel electric locomotive.

During the discovery sessions the instructor remained in the background, ready to answer questions, usually turning a question back to the questioner by inviting him to experiment further, giving no information himself.

The results of this work were strikingly in favour of the discovery method. Not only did the 'discovery' trainees have higher scores on tests than those trained by conventional classroom teaching, they also did so in half the time. Differences between older and younger trainees were smoothed out, in fact on one test the older men in the discovery group did much better than the younger men in the conventionally taught group. Similarly encouraging results have been obtained many times from experiments, where discovery methods were designed, for instance, to teach the skills of scribing a spanner or invisibly mending fine worsted cloth. The same sort of method was also used with success at Dublin airport, where an unskilled and largely poorly educated work force had to change from the comfortable muddle of the old system of freight storage to a modern computerized and completely automated one.

Application of the method

How is the discovery method applied? What are its most important stages and features?

1. The teacher starts with a careful analysis of the task, decides which are the most crucial elements, and cuts out or simplifies the rest.

2. Next he must somehow find out how the task looks to a learner. Where does a beginner start? What knowledge does he have already? What lack of knowledge is he covering up? The more expert an electrician or driver or upholsterer or dressmaker or

cook the teacher is, the harder it will be for him to see the difficulties of a subject as the learner sees them.

3. Having identified the learner's existing knowledge the teacher
then aims to build it up constantly, but in such a way that the
student can work unaided most of the time.

4. The teacher gives no direct instruction. He makes no attempt
to get his class to make or memorize notes or to listen to chalk-
and-talk lectures.

5. Instead the student works through sets of tasks, presented
through written or spoken instructions, inviting him to engage
in some carefully constructed and varied *activity*, usually a
slightly simplified version of the task in the real situation, i.e. he
is creating the experience he will use for learning.

6. The trainee observes and records the result of his actions and
is then asked questions, usually in writing, about the how and
why of what he has done. The method therefore emphasizes the
crucial importance of *understanding* in learning and depends on
challenging the learner to solve problems. Its success depends on
precisely gauging at what stage the student can solve which
problem, and on finding out how far the student can be pressed
to look for general patterns and rules.

Discovery learning in primary schools and in the early years
of the secondary school is perhaps more vague than this as yet,
but it is still recognizably the same process. In mathematics, for
instance, the children work in small groups, the teacher encourages them to take familiar materials like water or sand to weigh,
measure and pour, and from this to search for a hypothesis on
volume or area which can then be tested by more experiment for
its general truth. Newer methods of teaching languages, where
sentences are spoken, phrases used, actions performed and general
principles deduced later, might also be described as 'learning by
discovery', as could the recent emphasis in English teaching on
starting by creating or writing about a personal experience, however small, and worrying about punctuation, spelling and grammar only as they occur in each child's writing.

All these methods of discovery learning start by assuming that
the learner must actively create the experience through which he

learns and that the learner himself must deduce rules. Teachers using these methods do not start with idealized conceptions of what the bright child or perfectly skilled worker ought to be able to do.

Implications of the method

Many teachers of adults, both in industry and in adult education, are frightened by the implications of discovery learning. They tend to dismiss it as something good enough for young children or all right for those learning low-level skills in industry, but not applicable to their own particular subjects.

No one would suggest that any one teaching method would be appropriate for every sort of class, but discovery learning might well be applied to a wider range of educational situations than at first looks likely. For instance, in classes where aesthetic judgement is involved, it might seem difficult to devise a discovery situation, but in the class described below, the teacher had adopted a discovery method of learning with apparent success. The group consisted of teachers who were interested in producing amateur drama, but had no formal qualifications nor any previous experience of or aptitude for design. The subject of this part of the course was stage design:

The teacher did very little teaching as such. We spent all the available time doing things ourselves. This came as no particular surprise as we expected it to be practical. I suppose we did think we would be given some rules of thumb but none were promulgated at any time. Our first lessons were on basic elements of design. In the very first of these we arrived to find large pieces of paper and felt pens all laid out ready. Mr — explained that we were going to do an experiment to explore the relation between emotion and design. It had never occurred to most of us that there could be such a relation, and there were some scoffers! We were told how to divide our sheets into large grids and were then directed to the blackboard for further instructions. These were things like 'Draw horizontal lines a wide, even distance apart', or 'Draw diagonal lines close together'. When we had done several of these we were asked to look carefully at each one and to write at the side, without conferring with our neighbours, what emotions or feelings each set of lines suggested. We could write several for each grid. When we then discussed our suggestions, it was extraordinary how much they agreed. Maybe one person had written 'peace' for the horizontal lines, another 'monotony' and another 'depression', but the basic idea of a low-key, quiet emotion was the same. We later did the same kind of thing with shape (cut-out black shapes on white paper) and colour. We had a lot of quite exciting discussions in these classes and found we were able to carry through the ideas easily into our later work on actual stage design.

In this course it is noticeable that there is no suggestion of an aesthetic 'right answer'. 'Depression' was accepted along with 'peace' as a reasonable individual reaction to a set of horizontal lines. The class evidently accepted the method itself with equanimity, and it seems that the task, though extremely simple and streamlined, was still challenging enough to have provoked all the excitement and interest one would expect where people are exploring for themselves rather than being told. One can imagine the same approach adapted with very little difficulty for classes in interior design, flower arrangement, painting, sculpture, photography and fashion design, or indeed any subject which involved some element of aesthetic choice.

Advantages

This discovery type of learning undoubtedly has several tremendous advantages over more conventional classroom teaching. Because it avoids verbal instruction and demonstration, the learner does not have to make special efforts to memorize. People remember things most easily when they have been actively involved in them; by using the discovery method *every* student is actively involved *all* the time. There are none of those periods of desperate concentration on what the teacher is saying or doing, followed, especially in an evening class of tired people, by inevitable lapses of attention. There are no times when students need to scribble hasty notes which even they will read later with surprise. There is no need for the student to feel that apart from the few moments of private attention he receives from the tutor he might just as well be sitting at home painting or cooking or tinkering with his car.

Earlier chapters have attempted to show how diffident adult students may be in admitting that there is a process they have not understood. Indeed, adults may genuinely not see, or may find it hard to accept that they have misunderstood. Conventional teach-

ing techniques frequently help teacher and learner conspire together to cover up failure:

The do-it-yourself class was taken by a retired local builder. I remember the time we 'learnt' plastering. He'd just go sweeping up the
wall – 'Whoosh!' lovely. He talked all the time, but we were never
told exactly how to go 'whoosh' ourselves. However, he did pause
for a few seconds from time to time to say 'Any questions?' There
never were any. To answer our questions he'd have needed to go
right back to minus square one, and he made you feel he was going
to get through his syllabus or bust, so we let him get on with it,
nodding all the while as if we did understand. It was less trouble to
leave the class than to explain to him that he was going about fifty
times too fast.

Discovery methods, like programmed instruction, have the
merit that this sort of situation is impossible. If the piece of
learning is too hard, too fast or too dull for the capacities of the
learner, then these failings should be revealed immediately to
teacher and student. The work can then be re-planned. If the
pace, content and problem solving is just right, then the learner
has all the satisfaction of getting something right and of receiving
more or less instant knowledge of results. A teacher who works on
discovery lines and who starts from where the student is will
blame himself and his own planning if students fail; many
teachers in conventionally run classes start from where they
think the students ought to be and will blame them if this is a
standard they seem unable to reach.

It is important, in any case, for adults to be allowed to work
at their own pace. In a classroom where the emphasis is on the
teacher as expositer, demonstrator and star turn, this is only
rarely possible. Where the emphasis changes to the teacher as
resource-planner, the situation is very different. Discovery learning allows for the fact that people start with different kinds of
knowledge and work at different speeds. Work in pairs, as individuals, or in small groups becomes a viable possibility. The
teacher can spend his time on call as consultant, sorting out
particular difficulties as they arise. If there are always new sets
of work prepared, the teacher can direct different students to
start different tasks, so that in any one classroom there might be
several groups working happily on entirely different projects.

Discovery learning is based on the importance to the learner of understanding what he is doing. Tutors will occasionally say sourly of discovery methods that they cannot see the objection to *telling* people what to do, that it is 'easier' and 'quicker' to give them a few rules. It is true that it is bound to be much easier for the teacher to reel off rules or theories or information about techniques, but it is hardly ever easier for the learner. Learning involves first of all a slow grasp of a small part of a particular situation and only gradually a real understanding of general rules. Starting with the general rules may seem to cut corners, but it takes longer in the end.

Many teachers of leisure-subject classes have got away with expository methods for a long time because no one has tried to assess how much their classes have understood and are able to apply what they have learnt. This is the crunch. One cannot be said to have learnt how to bake a cake if one does not know what has gone wrong when the cake collapses in the oven; a painter will need to know not just how to mix colours but also why he achieves one particular colour with one particular mix of paints. Understanding in learning leads to flexibility when the learner comes to apply what he has learnt. In one of Dr Belbin's experiments the performance of a group of Swedish trainees taught to scribe a spanner by using programmed instruction was compared with the performance of those learning the same task through an instructor and through a discovery method. Although on written tests the discovery groups did not have outstanding results, when they came to apply what they had learnt in a final practical test they did very well, while the trainees in the other two groups slipped back into making elementary errors.

Sometimes the immediate results of a piece of teaching can be misleadingly good. People can cram for examinations and pass them well, but a few weeks later can have forgotten most of the facts they digested so rapidly; or can have buried themselves so deeply in preparing for particular questions that they have no general understanding of the subject at all. In industry there have been examples of beautiful training schemes developed to teach a rapid grasp of a particular task, where within a few years under pressure of technological change or consumer demand the task has altered and the training schemes have been useless. Teaching methods such as the discovery method concentrate on developing real understanding of a whole job rather than the highly specific processes of a particular task. They are thus much better suited to the swift pace of change of modern industry, where people like machinists may need to re-train every few years and to have flexible skills which are usable in the new situation.

Most groups of adults who have tried discovery learning seem to find it genuinely exciting and enjoyable. So far, the experimental evidence from work with adults shows that it is a method which seems to work particularly well with older adults and with those whose confidence, ability and experience in a formal learning situation is likely to be limited. However, there is no reason to suppose that given a sufficiently challenging piece of learning the method could not be developed to suit adult students right across the age and intelligence range. Certainly Nuffield discovery methods in mathematics and science have worked as well with bright sixth-formers as with average and below average primary-school children, because the intellectual appeal of experiment, and real open-endedness is irresistible.

Difficulties

It is true, however, that there are bound to be some students and some teachers who do not find the method pleasing. A teacher who likes to feel in complete personal control of everything that happens in his classroom, an authoritarian teacher, maybe even a nervous teacher, may reject discovery methods. Similarly, there will always be some students who want to be told, who would find it almost dishonest if the teacher asks the student to assemble an electrical circuit in order to learn about it when he could be so much more easily *told* what it is. In classes of grossly disparate ability this will be a problem, but it may be a challenge that also comes from a student whose ability is much like that of the rest of the class, but who feels for his own reasons insecure with discovery methods.

From the teacher's point of view the discovery method should never become fetishistic, plagued by an arid dogma of its own. There should be no temptation, for instance, to practise the dissembling of some primary-school teachers in dealing with children's questions. If a child asks 'What is a Prime Minister?' it is a poor reply to say 'I don't know, let's find out.' General questions should always be dealt with as they are raised, not by bland, closed replies, but in genuine discussion which invites further exploration and thought from the student and the group.

Resources

Discovery methods for adults have so far been used mostly for short pieces of specialized industrial training, where there has been no need for protracted teaching. A teacher in adult education wishing to adopt the method for a wider area would immediately come up against difficulties of time and money. Although in the classroom itself students can learn more quickly, the time needed by the teacher for preparation is greatly lengthened. Some discovery-type apparatus could be assembled quickly enough, but it is likely that providing something for each student for every lesson would cost more than many institutes could afford. Without magnificent and totally flexible resources it is likely, too, that discovery methods would need to be restricted to groups of students of roughly similar ability. The Nuffield mathematics and science solution has been to develop national resources which individual teachers can then call on. Perhaps the same approach will eventually be adopted for the commonly taught subjects in adult education. Until then, discovery learning is likely to remain an occasional strategy for short, sharp use rather than a normal way of learning.

Programmed instruction

In the first few years of its life programmed instruction quickly became associated in teachers' minds with unpleasant images of what they fervently prayed education would not become: arid, dehumanized, perhaps super-efficient, but deadly dull. The early connections of the method with teaching machines were unfortunate. A teaching machine seemed to many teachers to be a contradiction in terms; more than that, it undoubtedly brought out the Luddite in some teachers who, not surprisingly, feared for their jobs, in view of the extravagant claims made by some of the early protagonists of programmed instruction.

Now that programmed instruction is older and wiser it no longer seems so threatening, because few people would claim for it any godlike potentiality in education. Paradoxically it appears more limited in many ways than was originally thought, but at the same time it now seems to offer far greater opportunities for blending flexibly with a variety of other media and methods.

Modern programmed instruction is now very similar to many sorts of discovery learning, and the principles on which discovery learning is based and designed could equally well apply to programmed instruction. The differences now are really ones of emphasis, of historical development, of resources and research effort. Programmed instruction is now a specialism which is rapidly becoming more esoteric, while discovery learning still seems within the grasp of the amateur.

The theory

The theory behind programmed instruction was simple enough: it was that learning happens most effectively when the task to be learned is analysed, broken down into very small units, and presented to the learner in a logical sequence at a pace he can control himself, and in such a way that he nearly always achieves the right answer. Each unit or frame of the programme contains both information and a question – sometimes new information and new questions, sometimes simply repeating and rounding up what the student has already learnt. The student generally checks himself on whether or not he has the right answer before continuing to the next frame.

It is this step-by-step response which makes programmed instruction different from just reading a well-planned book or listening to an excellent lecture – both of which might fulfil some of the conditions described above. Supporters of the method claim that by actively involving the learner in discovering for himself whether he has understood each fragment of knowledge, in a well-designed programme not only does he have the pleasure – reinforcement – of achieving right answers, but he and his teacher have immediate checks on his progress. It is one of the basic priciples of programmed instruction that a programme is tested before being put into general use and that if the preliminary tests reveal that the learners are making a large number of mistakes then the fault lies with the programme writer, who must alter his programme accordingly.

There are two main types of programme, 'branching' and 'linear'.

Branching programmes

Branching programmes work by presenting the student with a piece of information and then offering a set of alternative answers. If a question is asked giving three alternative choices of answer and C is the right answer, then a student choosing A or B, the wrong answers, would be taken to a 'remedial' frame in which the original material would be explained again. The student choosing C would press on through the main teaching sequence. If the programme is being presented on a teaching machine, the student presses the button marked A, B or C according to his answer, and the new frame appears on the screen automatically. A simpler, less expensive way of achieving the same effect is to use a scrambled book where the pages are in deliberate numerical disorder to prevent cheating. The student is directed to different pages according to the answer he chooses.

A branching sequence from a programmed book, intended for sixth-formers or first-year undergraduates is reproduced here to show how the actual frames of a scrambled sequence work out. The sequence comes from an early part of the programme, where the scope and meaning of 'psychology' is being explained.*

From page 5   6

The study of abnormal behaviour is part of psychology – again, to the extent that this behaviour is studied scientifically. Psychology is concerned with all kinds of behaviour, normal and abnormal. The study of abnormal behaviour is sometimes called 'abnormal psychology'.

Would you go further than this and say that, for all practical purposes, the study of abnormal behaviour was the main interest of most psychologists?

8 Yes

11 No

From page 6   8

'Most psychologists are mainly interested in abnormal behaviour,' you say. But what makes you say this?

I expect you are getting mixed up between psychology and

*Michael J. Apter, An Introduction to Psychology, Teaching Programmes Ltd, Bristol, 1965.

'*Psychiatry*'. This is indeed a very common mistake among people who have not had the opportunity of seriously studying psychology, but who have managed to pick up a little information from newspapers and magazines. The man who asks his patients to lie down on a couch and talk to him is not a psychologist but a psychiatrist. (Note also that psychiatrists are in any case becoming less and less like the popular image as more and more is understood of the physiological basis of mental disturbance.)

Turn to page 9

From page 8   9

Thus only a few psychologists, comparatively speaking, are directly interested in abnormal behaviour, whereas this is the sole interest of psychiatrists.

It might appear from this that psychiatry is a part of psychology and that abnormal psychology is identical with psychiatry. But this would not be true. Psychology is interested in *understanding* behaviour, including abnormal behaviour, psychiatry is interested in *treating* abnormal behaviour.

What is the common ground between abnormal psychology and psychiatry?

Turn to page 7

From page 9/11   7
ABNORMAL BEHAVIOUR

We can say that psychology is part of *science*, since it is concerned with finding out about the way things are; psychiatry is part of *medicine*, since it is concerned with treating people when something is wrong with them.

They are closely related since, in order to cure something, the more one knows about it the better. Thus, in principle, psychology is the science (along with physiology) on which psychiatry is based.

Psych—s are scientists, psych—s are doctors.

Turn to page 10

From page 6   11

No, of course most psychologists are not mainly interested in abnormal behaviour. This is only one kind of behaviour, interesting as it is.

It is, however, worth noticing an important distinction; that between psychology and '*Psychiatry*'. For the psychiatrist is solely interested in abnormal behaviour. He differs from the psychologist in that the psychologist is trying to understand behaviour (and the abnormal psychologist is trying to *understand* abnormal behaviour), whereas the psychiatrist *treats* abnormal behaviour.

What is the common ground between abnormal psychology and psychiatry?

Turn to page 7

From page 7   10

PsychOLOGISTS are scientists, psychIATRISTS are doctors.

Psychology and psychiatry are also related in that information about what psychiatric treatments have been found to be successful can help the psychologist the better to understand abnormal behaviour.

There is also a branch of psychology called '*clinical psychology*', which is part of *applied psychology*. This is not concerned with understanding the behaviour of patients in mental hospitals and clinics (this would be abnormal psychology), nor in curing this behaviour (which would be psychiatry), but with aiding the psychiatrist in the practical task of testing and diagnosing patients as a preliminary to treatment.

What is the difference between clinical psychology, abnormal psychology and psychiatry?

Turn to page 12

Branching programmes can become extremely complicated both to write and to use if they have endless remedial frames, but their theoretical advantage is that they offer the student opportunities for further explanation and trial in those parts of the subject in which he is most uncertain.

At their best, branching programmes offer a sensitive way of adapting learning to individual needs; at their worst the poorer branching programmes have suffered from a sense that they were introducing needless complication, suggesting wrong answers, creating confusions where none previously existed in the learner's mind (though, of course, where the programme writer has accurately identified confusions, this is no longer a valid criticism). Some people also found that the common methods of presentation caused difficulty. Teaching machines, apparently the neatest way of using a branching programme, are expensive and can normally only be used by one person at a time. Furthermore, their one advantage, preventing the student from cheating, now seems to be of dubious merit when experience has shown that students enjoy the chance to look back over previous frames or look forward to coming frames and learn just as well when allowed to do so.

Scrambled books have the same disadvantage; some people also found it irritating to use books which had been too enthusiastically scrambled and which needed constant page-flicking in use.

Linear programmes

In a *linear* programme progress is uncomplicated by branches, the programme is designed so that it can be worked right through, though, like a branching programme, it can incorporate 'skip' frames, when a student who has achieved excellent results on a halfway test can be directed to skip one section of the programme. Another major difference from a branching programme is that the student makes a different sort of response, called in the jargon a 'constructed response', to the question asked after new material is presented. This means that instead of being offered three or four possible answers to the question, the student has to invent the answer himself. Thus a few frames from a home-made linear programme, used with a masking card on the right-hand side of the page, on job evaluation for shop stewards took this form. Its long answers are rather untypical of the linear form.

Job evaluation is a way of trying to find a fair rate for a job. It has nothing to do with people with stopwatches assessing individuals. Is job evaluation the same thing as time-and-motion study?	
Job evaluation is also concerned with assessing one job in relation with another. The result of a job-evaluation exercise is usually a system of grades. After job evaluation has been carried out, workers doing similar jobs are likely to be paid on the same —.	No. Job evaluation is a way of looking at a type of job. It is the job which is assessed, not the individual doing it.

One way of carrying out job evaluation is a system of 'job ranking', where each job is put in order of importance.	Grades
In a small factory there are these jobs, among others: driver, fitter, floor-sweeper, progress-chaser, storekeeper.	
Place them in rank order. Do you think your judgement would be reliable?	

	It might be, it might not be. Most people would rank those jobs like this:
	
	   Progress-chaser
	   Fitter
	   Storekeeper
	   Driver
	   Floor-sweeper
	
	but without knowing more about the factory, it would be difficult to be certain.

In its most pure and typical form the linear programme might help the student by offering enormous clues to the right answer – perhaps leaving only part of the word blank – but in more sophisticated forms, the 'right' answer might be more open-ended, something much nearer to the principles of discovery learning.

The simplest way of using a linear programme is to set it out in book form, but to print the answers in a right-hand margin which is covered by a masking card moved down the page by the student. Some linear programmes in book form are printed with only one frame on each page, so that the student always has to turn the page before reading the answer.

Linear programmes can also be used with machines. Although there are sophisticated, streamlined linear machines on the market, many teachers have developed perfectly satisfactory home-made versions which do the same job – basically, to allow the programme to be written on a long roll of paper which passes an opening, where the student both reads the frame and writes his response. These home-made machines often look like large box-cameras, with two rollers to hold the programme.

The developing debate

In its early days there were fierce battles between rival academic camps, each determined to prove that a linear programme was intrinsically superior to a branching programme, or vice versa. There was a good deal of debate too on whether responses were better written, spoken or merely *thought*; on whether there was an ideal, magic number of words per frame. Today not only has it been realized that the distinction between branching and linear programmes can be blurred, there is also a growing realization that there can be no single ideal type of programme, that different programmes will suit different situations. For instance, an undergraduate might prefer a linear programme with frames of up to three hundred words, an engineering apprentice using a programme to learn the use of a milling machine might do better with frames a sixth of that size. One might also tentatively suggest that a simple linear programme is probably best suited to groups whose members are of much the same ability, and who are at the beginning of learning some rudimentary skill or set of concepts to which it is possible to give straightforward right or wrong answers. A branching programme might be more likely to suit a group of more mixed ability, where there is also a wider range of initial knowledge of the topic to be learned, where the subject-matter will respond more to being teased out, and where the programmer's suggestions can be tested against the conclusions the student forms for himself. Even these distinctions are crude. The needs of the class and the quality and type of the programmes used can only be judged in each individual case to give the best result. Careful analysis of what is to be learnt is more important than slavish adherence to one type of programme.

Some other treasured ideas of the pioneers of programmed instruction have been eroded in the light of further research – for

instance, the vision of the student working through his programme in a lonely booth by himself, at his own pace. It was this
idea of the solitary student which aroused much of the orginal
irritated opposition to programmed instruction. Many teachers
stressed the value to the individual of working in a group. Slowly,
research has established what teachers have felt they always knew
by instinct anyway – that students enjoy working with one
another, that group discussion is a valuable way of reinforcing
or testing out what one has just learnt, that other people's contributions can add a spice to one's own.

A variety of uses

The result has been that although programmed instruction is
still probably used most commonly by individuals who work
together but separately, starting and finishing at different times,
it is also increasingly used in varied group situations. One such
situation is a classroom where the students sit round a table
watching a screen showing slides or film which gives some of
the material to be learnt, linked with printed pages which ask
multiple-choice questions. The student chooses an answer and
presses one of four buttons in front of him. These link with a
console on the teacher's desk and will show and record at a glance
which and how many students have got the right answer. The
film or slides can be stopped at any time for discussion.

Although this system has drawbacks, notably that for adults it
may introduce an undesirable competitive element, it does also
have considerable advantages over conventional programmed
instruction because it offers opportunities for introducing a
variety of media. There was much justified criticism of the dull-
ness and poor quality of writing of many early attempts at programmed instruction. The programmes had, and many still have,
a doughy quality which comes from over-dependance on badly
written prose. Group systems offering possibilities for economical
use of tape, slides, television and film are promising ways of adding a bit of necessary yeast to presentation.

The early faith of the programmers that the student could
work best in splendid independence of the teacher has proved to
be another false trail. Certainly programmes can and do teach
more than adequately. Many programmes by themselves have

been shown to teach successfully, perhaps more so than many teachers teaching in the conventional way. But recent research suggests more and more strongly that it is programme *plus* teacher which gives better results than either programme alone or teacher alone.

This is perhaps not a surprising result. Early programmes attempted to replace the teacher in the student's mind with often comically insincere and syrupy praise or carefully toned-down criticism. Phrases like 'Very good – you have got the right answer' or 'No, not quite, I should think you must have confused ...' seasoned the frames, even though experience suggested that simply knowing whether the answer was right or wrong worked just as well. Now, with the sanction of research and experiment, the programme writers can happily leave the personal encouragement to the teacher.

Changes in approach

There have been changes, too, in subject-matter and approach. It is true that the great majority of published programmes are still entirely in written form, rely on some kind of verbal response, and tend to concern subjects such as mathematics or science with an easily analysed logical core. However, even in these subjects, more programmes in recent years are incorporating activity, experiment and problem solving. For instance, in this simple home-made programme, with each frame duplicated on strips of paper and clipped together, experiment, activity and teacher cooperation is built in to a linear programme.

A Model of Molecular Motion in Gases

Instructions

1. Read each page *carefully*, trying to remember the important points. You may be required to recollect them when reading other parts of this booklet.
2. Follow the instructions for the experiment in the order given.
3. At the bottom of most pages there is a question for you to answer. Think out your answer *before* turning to the next page.
4. Check your answer at the top of the next page before reading on. Your answer may not correspond exactly to the one given but it should mean the same thing.

5. If you disagree with the answer given then go back and read the page once more and repeat that part of the experiment. If you still disagree then consult the teacher.

1. For this model you require a small tray with upright sides containing twenty small glass marbles. One of these marbles must be a different colour but the same size as the others. The bottom of the tray is lined with soft cork to reduce the noise made by the marbles rolling around in the tray.

2. The simplest method of operating the model is to put the tray flat on a table or on the floor and rapidly shake the tray so that it moves in small circles. The marbles will then move around in a haphazard way, bumping into each other and the sides of the tray.

If you have difficulty in doing this ask the teacher for some help and advice.

3. Try to watch the marble which is different in colour as it moves around the tray.

When does it change its direction of movement?

4. The marble changes direction only when it bounces off the sides of the tray or off another marble. Between these collisions it will travel in a straight line. If you have difficulty in seeing this, try shaking the tray a little less quickly.

Watch the marble again and see if you can predict in which direction it will go after a collision or which marble it will bump into next.

5. No, it seems to be completely unpredictable. The collisions are so rapid that the movement appears to be completely haphazard.

Does the speed of the marble change when it bumps into another marble? If so can you predict whether it will go faster or slower?

6. Yes, the speed usually seems to change when it bounces into another marble. Occasionally it is possible to notice that when it is moving quickly and hits a slower moving marble it will be slowed down and vice versa, but making predictions is very difficult.

Does the marble seem to travel the same distance each time between one collision and the next?

7. No. This is completely random and unpredictable, too. It is impossible to predict its speed, direction or distance moved after any collision.

Is this also true for the other marbles? Shake the tray again and watch the motion of some of these other marbles.

8. Yes. These marbles are also moving around in an unpredictable way. Each marble moves in a different direction but they all have a random motion. The distinctive marble is typical of all the others.

Try to make a rough drawing of the movements of the distinctive marble showing how far it moves in each direction and its changes of direction.

Changes in subject-matter

Mathematics and science are still most easily coped with by teaching programmes, but more and more programmes are being attempted in craft or skill subjects or in elusive subjects such as management training, involving delicate judgements previously thought to be resistant to a programmed approach. More importantly perhaps, instead of being a method to be rigidly advocated in all circumstances, programmed instruction can now be seen as a useful part of a much broader canvas of classroom activity, at one time forming the centre of work for every student for a longish patch of time, at another offering a useful way for a newcomer to catch up. In other circumstances it might simply give a skeletal framework which can occasionally fill in some missing links for those who need them, but more usually simply direct a much more wide-ranging set of activities and problems through which a student works at his own pace.

Advantages

The advantages of programmed instruction when used as flexibly as this will be so similar to the advantages of the discovery method described earlier in this chapter that they need little further elaboration: all the students will be actively involved; they can work at their own pace either individually or in groups; since the programme will have been tried and tested, most of them should learn rapidly and accurately. Like discovery learning, programmed instruction should open the way to much more flexible teaching units. Teachers freed from their role of giving out information to twenty or so students simultaneously can become coordinators, consultants, people who make learning happen without having to attempt to supervise personally each step for each student all of the time. The group of twenty conducted by one teacher is no longer a necessity. Two teachers can work together in a team-teaching situation with perhaps sixty or seventy students, who would sometimes come together for a film or lecture, at other times split into very small groups of three or four.

However, it is hard to make sweeping gestures of approval or disapproval of programmed instruction now, as it is rapidly coming to take as many forms as there are teaching situations. The old, dull peck-peck-peck approach to learning is being replaced by a much more flexible set of systems which only have their rigorous analysis, careful planning and testing in common with the early attempts. Even so, it is bound to be the case that many teachers will reject even this freer form of programming.

Some criticism by teachers of programmed instruction has been ludicrously emotional, demanding criteria and standards of proof which such teachers had clearly never applied to their own work. Other teachers have felt that programmed instruction may well be a promising approach to education, but feel that they could not cope with the different set of classroom skills it demands, or that the technique is still too limited in its application.

No teaching system can or should be applied wholesale. Much research and effort is currently going into programmed instruction and it seems likely that many developments will give it tremendous possibilities – for instance, for linking it with computers which can record each student's progress and offer finely judged individual work assignments and new pieces of learning. Even so, computer-assisted instruction must seem like so much pie in the sky to many teachers of adults. In industry, it is true, programmed instruction is already widely used, and the question is not so much 'Should we use it?' as 'How much and where should we use it?' It looks as if computer-assisted instruction will eventually follow the same pattern.

Problems for the teacher

The situation for teachers of adults in the much more impoverished evening institutes is quite different. There is neither time to write and test programmes on students nor money to buy commercially published versions. Constantly shifting emphases of interest and ability would make this a difficult task anyway. A part-time teacher earning under £3 for two hours' teaching would need to be extraordinarily dedicated to write, test, re-write and print enough programmed material to last his class throughout the year. For this sort of teacher, an occasional use of a particular programme is all he could hope for.

If he wanted to write his own programme he would be up against a more serious drawback. Programmed instruction has in only a short time accumulated a vast literature, a rich dogma, a lot of jargon, and many beautiful, complex rules on how to write a programme. Different sects at different universities will offer different and often conflicting advice. This is the price paid for the imaginative hold which programmed instruction has inspired and for the quantity of research which has emerged – it has become increasingly difficult for an amateur to write his own programme because academics are constantly refining and re-shaping the programme writer's tools. There are some good introductory guides, notably the work of Kay, Dodd and Sime,* but it seems to be one of the dangers of current trends in programmed instruction that a race of professional programmers will emerge, and that the ordinary teacher who knows his ordinary students through and through will be deterred from writing the sort of excellent tailor-made programme only he could achieve.

Many teachers feel dubious about how their students will react to programmed instruction. One reason it has been possible to use the technique so widely and, as it turned out, so successfully in industry and in the armed forces has undoubtedly been the more certain control the industrial or military trainer has over his class. He has fewer fears that his class will rebel, politely or openly, about his methods. They are much more likely to accept the techniques he offers and it is not nearly so easy for them to protest by simply not turning up to the next class. They know there is a body of knowledge they must acquire and are often willing to take the teacher's word about what is likely to be the shortest route.

The teacher in the gentler atmosphere of voluntary adult education may face a quite different situation, and whether or not he uses programmed instruction must be a more delicate decision.

*Harry Kay, Bernard Dodd and Max Sime, *Teaching Machines and Programmed Instruction*, Penguin, 1968.

He may feel that his students have a distorted picture of programmed instruction, and that they may resist its introduction in
the classroom. Only he and they can judge whether a programme
and what kind of programme might work well. Clearly the first
job such a programme must do is to convince the students
straight away that they can learn from it.

Other teachers feel more fundamental doubts about the extent
to which programmed instruction can be applied at the moment.
They feel, perhaps rightly, that programmed instruction is
most suitable for simple stages of learning where it can still be
said that there is a 'right' answer. They will reject programmed
instruction as they will reject certain kinds of guided-discovery
learning, because they feel that these methods appear to rule
straight lines into a piece of learning, to lay down its structure
too closely, and to cut out the possibility of serendipity – the gift
of making happy discoveries by chance. This is a cogent, serious
criticism for at the moment too few programmes and too few
research projects have been designed to teach creativity, or to
suggest how far programmed instruction can explore and indeed to create areas of doubt and uncertainty. These are problems for the future.

Chapter 8
Projects

Project work has been around a long time in schools. From being something daring and innovatory it has now become almost a cliché, in many cases earning itself a bad name for being an excuse for the teacher to have a quiet nap while the children are tucked away in the library copying out half-digested pieces from encyclopedias, doing individual projects on sixteenth-century armour or timber-framed-houses-through-the-ages.

In adult education, on the other hand, the project is still in its prime and as a means of learning by doing and of teaching by investigation has developed in different ways. Far from being the occasion for the feats of individual academic virtuosity which the school-type project encourages at its best and lamentably fails to encourage at its worst, the adult-education project has become a way for the individual to learn within the group and for the group to learn from the community.

It is at this point of contact with the community that the adult-education project has had its most significant impact. Project work usually involves the group leaving the cocoon of the classroom and venturing out to seek raw materials from local people, records or conditions. Even where the materials have not been local, but have involved the group in an intensive study of some foreign or national event, the result of the project, its end product, has often been in a form which involved offering something to the community – a book, an exhibition, a series of study walks, a play.

Scope of the project method

Two classic studies, both sociological and undertaken by adult-education classes in Nottingham and Basingstoke, show something of the characteristic scope and impact of the project method. In Nottingham a group of twenty students under the leadership of two tutors from the university, Ken Coates and

Richard Silburn, made a study of the St Ann's district of the town, uncovering widespread material deprivation, desperately poor housing, low aspiration and poor educational achievement.* The group, which began as a normal course in sociology, turned itself over three years into a highly efficient research team as well as continuing, as an adult-education group, to learn a good deal at a high conceptual level about social class in general, poverty in general and sociology in general. One of the students, Rosalind Kent, describes the personal impact the work had on her :

The area itself was ugly, dirty and depressing to work in and, on occasion, a little frightening. Having felt my way, one dark night, from an alleyway down a long backyard, I arrived to find the house derelict and, suddenly, the next-door neighbour shining a torch into my face and inquiring what I was up to.

Some of the families I interviewed were living in conditions of extreme discomfort; rotten house fabric, ill-fitting draughty windows, very damp walls, outside toilets, no hot-water systems or bathrooms and overcrowding were common facts of life. One particular family I remember was afflicted with all these ills and the mother had to share a bedroom with the daughter as this was the only means of giving her any privacy. Another woman had nursed a dying husband under these conditions and without realizing that she was entitled to sickness benefits. . . .

Of course as our survey progressed so did the spirit of teamwork and *camaraderie*. This had nothing to do with the fact that our gathering-point after a strenuous evening's interviewing was often a strategic pub.

After the interviewing was over, I was left with a sense of guilt, each time, on returning to my own cosy middle-class home. . . .†

The sense of indignation and surprise in this description, typical of the way the group and the tutors felt about what they were learning, was bound to seep through the apparently neutral, unemotional and well-illustrated report the group produced. The local impact was tremendous. Some members of the council felt

* Ken Coates and Richard Silburn, 'St Ann's : poverty, deprivation and morale in a Nottingham community', Nottingham University Department of Adult Education, 1967.

† Rosalind Kent, 'Not for ostriches', *W E A News*, March 1968.

that what the group had uncovered was bound to be interpreted as an assault on their policies and efficiency. The group was attacked, often abusively, for seeming to be snoopers, or for exaggerating; other local people felt some of the outrage the group itself had felt about conditions in St Ann's, and were disturbed at the implications of the report. However the survey results are interpreted, it is surely right that a local community, and indeed a national one, should be aware of and should discuss something so important as the possibility of there being extensive poverty in its midst, and right also, that the question can be raised by a group of people from the community itself who are at the same time engaged in serious learning within and through it.

In Basingstoke, on a less combustible subject, the WEA was involved almost from the start in plans to expand the town from being a small market town 26,000 strong to an overspill giant of 85,000. Starting in 1960 a series of classes studied and obtained new facts about innumerable aspects of the town's character, pouring out a stream of information at all sorts of levels, some of it aimed at academics engaged in town expansion and planning problems elsewhere, some of it amusing lighthearted reading, some simply designed to keep local people informed of developments to prepare them for the future and to invite them to participate in planning it.

Projects have long tentacles. A WEA class in Herefordshire and Shropshire studying Offa's Dyke offered back some of its knowledge in the form of public 'summer-study walks', gave talks to branches of local archaeological societies, ran coach excursions, and became involved in negotiations to reopen rights of way over those parts of the Dyke which had become impenetrable jungles. An Offa's Dyke Action Committee was formed, maps of routes were made and distributed, guidebooks were written for people who wished to follow the routes. It is often the case that when after such projects the class itself has been wound up, and the members have learned a considerable amount of archaeology or sociology, the effectiveness of the work is continued by formation of a local pressure-group or society. Much of the detailed archaeological and social history of Britain has been rediscovered and rewritten since the Second World War by societies of this type, which had their origin in an adult-education group which had stepped outside the self-absorption of the conventional class.

In all these projects the classes have not simply been the cheap, amateur means of making a survey necessarily a form of sociological self-help in less centralized, sparsely populated parts of Australia or the United States. They have also been a serious method of learning for members of the groups, who through active involvement have perhaps been able to grasp tougher academic nettles than a class covering the same ground in a more passive way.

Opportunities for learning

Groups engaging on project work are as likely as members of other adult classes to be mixed in ability, confidence and experience. Project work, expertly managed, seems uniquely well suited to allow each member of the group to find his own level quietly at first, and then to seize opportunities for learning which might have seemed to present formidable obstacles if demanded of the same student in a conventional class. In theory there might be dangers of a few confident and assertive members of the group engaging for themselves all the more 'interesting' tasks and surging ahead while the rest of the group splashes round still in the shallows. In practice this does not often seem to happen. Tutors who have led groups working on projects will frequently remark that if the project grips the interest of the group, it seems only a matter of time before every member of it makes some quite startling leap forward. It could be the shy housewife, apparently too timid to take part in the ordinary interviewing for a social survey, who suddenly volunteers to interview a notoriously prickly member of the local council. It could be the even shyer class member who stays silent through almost every class meeting, but who accepts without question that he will lead a study walk around an old fortress which the group is excavating, or that he will take his share of the lecturing engagements which come the way of the class through local interest which the project has aroused.

The opportunities which a project offers to work with the group, but as a free agent inside it, also seems to stimulate a surprising amount of individual academic initiative. For instance, in one group of day-release students, many of whom had done no formal academic work for fifteen years or more, several students on different occasions appeared in the class with papers prepared on the results of research they had undertaken entirely on their own initiative. One such piece was a detailed and scholarly appraisal of all known sources of information on local pits since the fourteenth century, another was a survey of the history of the village since the Domesday Book which drew on over twenty separate original sources. The only previous pieces of written work either of these students had done were half-page accounts, clearly written with difficulty, of the state of wage negotiations in one coal mine.

Indeed, the whole tormented 'problem' of wringing 'written work' out of students fades away in the context of a project. It is not at all surprising that teachers often find it hard to persuade students to write essays. Children may accept with comparative docility that one of the ways of learning is to shape recently acquired knowledge into a one-thousand-word form with paragraphs, a beginning, a middle and an end, which is then appraised by the teacher. It is not surprising that adults resist what must appear to be a stereotyped presentation, artificial in the context of an adult class which is not going to be examined in the essay form and therefore sees no reason to practise it.

Written work is, of course, a valuable way of learning, but it is only one among many ways – discussing, listening, thinking – of sifting, constructing and presenting an argument, and it does not have to take the classical essay form. In the course of a project, most of the group members will at some time do an extended piece of writing, which could well be more taxing to them than any essay, but its shape might be a simple duplicated sheet containing a few terse highlights, the fruits of a long, detailed piece of research into local wills, parish records and electoral registers, or it might be a paper formally written after an extensive reading programme and then delivered to the rest of the group, giving a god's-eye view of all the major academic writing on, say, Roman Britain or social class.

The difference between this sort of work and the normal essay is that students approach it for a different purpose. The delights of writing a good essay are normally the private and individual sense of pleasure produced by having tidied one corner of knowledge to one's own satisfaction. The motivation and reward is confined to this perhaps ritualistic transaction between teacher and student. With written work produced as part of a project there is the additional spur that it is being produced out of necessity: the rest of the group really needs to know what one has discovered. A piece of entirely new information or a cogent survey of other people's information researched and assessed on one's own for this purpose takes on an altogether different flavour, because the need to communicate it to other people is more intense.

Varieties of method

Then, too, the end product itself, and the very fact that there is to be an end product, may well mean that each member of the group has to produce more written work, and to a higher standard, than might be demanded in a conventional class. Some tutors write up the final report themselves, others act as editors or hand over the task completely to one or more members of the group. The procedure, like the form of the report itself, will depend on the group and on the task. Some reports have been duplicated sheets stapled together, distributed at a nominal price. Others have been simple pamphlets, but beautifully printed and illustrated.* The form need not be stereotyped. Indeed one major survey may be a fruitful and continuous source of varied end-product material – handouts, printed pamphlets, books, lectures and films, or even a documentary novel with several authors. The Basingstoke WEA's involvement in the plans for the town has among other things meant the production of a sixpenny pamphlet containing a collection of lighthearted quotations about the town, 'The Things They Say about Basingstoke'; a short pamphlet reporting on facilities in the town, 'Basingstoke – A Social Study'; a solid academic case study of town expansion, *Economic Planning and Town Expansion* by John Dunning, one of the teachers who led the group;† and a history of the town

* For example, *Hatfield and its People*, 12 vols., Hatfield WEA, 1959–64.
† John Dunning, *Economic Planning and Town Expansion*, Southampton WEA, 1963.

prepared as a tape-slide presentation, with a commentary spoken by John Arlott, which has already been lent out to audiences totalling well over five thousand people.

It is a pity that this last type of enterprise is still so rare. Maybe it is the long years of fretting over the quantity of their students' written work, maybe it is the still prevalent belief that the printed word is somehow superior to the spoken or recorded word, but most groups have chosen print for their end products. Admirably professional and thorough though most of these have been, it seems a pity that more adult groups have not also experimented with film, with drama (improvised or carefully written and re-hearsed), or with closed-circuit television. Expense might pre-clude elaborate film and television work, but improvised drama certainly need not be costly, and facilities for sound recording are within every group's grasp. Indeed now that there are so many local radio stations all eager for material, radio pro-grammes will be perhaps the most natural way of communicating the first findings of a project group.

The more varied the forms of presentation, the more oppor-tunities and challenges it will offer the members of the group for learning. Someone whose written work is poor may yet make a superbly informal and articulate radio presenter; the person who may not be entirely happy working on academic research may have a flair for its accurate and readable presentation in short articles for the local press. Other members of the group may have the creative skills in artwork or photography, invaluable in preparing material for printing or in mounting an exhibition.

Using existing skills

In this way projects offer not only the opportunities for develop-ing new skills but also the chance to utilize old ones for the benefit of the group. Much noise is made in adult education about something normally known as 'using the experience and talents of the student', but it is rare for a teacher to be able to do very much more than simply offer concepts to the group for them to sieve through their own experience. Many of the generalizations, for instance, of sociologists and historians rightly prove too coarse for the exacting judgements made by members of adult classes, who are often less ready to accept such generalizations than young students. Teachers and students can feel happy that in these circumstances the student's life experience has been 'used' to the satisfaction of both. This is, of course, a valuable educational process as well as a courtesy due to adults by right. However, in a project, the student's professional skills as well as his general experience can become absolutely vital to the group. Here, for instance, in an extract from a paper by the two Nottingham tutors Coates and Silburn, is an example of how the composition and character of the class and the skills of its individual members affected the work the Nottingham group was able to do in its investigation of the St Ann's district.

When the class assembled in October, it had attracted twenty registrations, including a number of people with a professional interest in the chosen area, some of whom had access to facts, records and statistics which are not generally available. There were three probation officers, a schoolteacher who was married to an immigrant and who lived on the border of the area, an accountant in the corporation's housing department, two journalists, a charge-hand in a local factory who also served on its sick and benevolent fund committee, three secretarial employees, an architect in the employ of the city council, an accountant in private employment, and a number of housewives. Many of these people were able to set up separate but parallel investigations into the records of their own departments, thus producing a number of related profiles of the chosen area. Thus we obtained precise records of juvenile offenders in the area, of youth-club facilities, of houses in the area which were owned by the corporation, of rateable values of industrial and commercial establishments within the area, and of some of the major complaints about overall living conditions within it. Other investigations whose results were keenly awaited included a detailed study of the educational needs of the area, and of the attainments of its children.

Other students who had not the advantage of access to otherwise restricted information were nonetheless able to make significant contributions to our knowledge of the area: for instance, one student completed a detailed survey of inward and outward mobility, street by street, from electoral registers chosen at an interval of four years. A number of students examined and priced the diet set out by Rowntree and Lavers in their classic *Poverty and the Welfare State*, revealing very wide discrepancies between price levels in city-centre supermarkets and local corner shops, to the considerable disadvantage of the corner shops. One keen student even went so far as to feed her family on the Rowntree and Lavers 1951 diet for a week, during which time they ingested not only a fair quantity of sago and lentils, but also six pounds of swedes. She reported that they were all relieved when the experiment was successfully concluded.*

The interdisciplinary factor

Much lip service is paid today to the value of interdisciplinary studies, but the majority of teachers continue, understandably enough, to plough their lonely geographical, historical or literary furrows. To do anything else may be too time consuming and simply too difficult for one teacher alone. One of the strengths and at the same time, of course, one of the potential weaknesses of project work is that such straitness is virtually impossible. Because the findings themselves are by definition unknown to the teacher as well as to the group, there is no knowledge to be neatly parcelled up and presented in isolation. As soon as a group starts work on a project the boundaries of knowledge inevitably split and become blurred. For instance, a rural group whose members begin by studying local history, involving as they think the medieval church, the wool trade and the later local industries, might very well find themselves driven to looking as well at geography and geology to explain how it was that the wool trade grew up in the first place. They might also need to know some natural history to examine the ecological structure of the area, some archaeology to have a closer look at local remains, some demography to seek for explanations of change in population, to say nothing of sociology when it came to comparing the past with the present.

Even a simple sociological project will most probably involve practising the social skills of interviewing, the literary skills of presenting information in agreeable form, as well as reading up the appropriate historical and literary background. The inter-disciplinary skills acquired are not always intellectual ones. As part of one project an archaeological group felt obliged to build a medieval kiln in which they experimented with the production of thirteenth- and fourteenth-century glazed wares, while

*Ken Coates and Richard Silburn, 'Urban renewal: a social survey', *Adult Education*, vol. 40, no. 3, 1967.

another group found and rebuilt an early steam engine as part of an investigation in industrial archaeology.

The larger view

One of the potential dangers of a project is undoubtedly that the group can bury itself so deep in local or intensively small issues that it can overlook the large ones, or fail to see where the links between local and national, minor and major developments can be made. It is clearly the teacher's job to see that these links are made in a meaningful way. Some projects have begun because the groups themselves had failed to understand the large picture, or else simply did not believe it – the Nottingham group, for instance, started with a course on the 'Anatomy of Britain', and only found it a credible idea that $7\frac{1}{2}$ million people in Britain could be living in virtual poverty when they began to investigate the poverty on their own doorsteps. It was natural then in this survey for the group to be constantly driven back to the national picture as a yardstick for their local one. Such information needed to be acquired more urgently than it might have been in a class which had continued as a course of lectures. A class in this situation can accept a far more rigorous academic treatment, either from its own teacher or from a visiting specialist, than the constantly boiled-down fare it might more usually be offered, where the temptation to regurgitate received opinions and fifth-hand information is often too strong for a teacher to resist.

Furthermore, the process of having been involved themselves in making knowledge-sifting opinions, constructing questionnaires, excavating archaelogical sites, examining documentation, searching through other people's arguments and then constructing an argument oneself, gives students an altogether different way of looking at other people's work. The student who has himself helped construct a survey will know how important the phrasing of questions in the interview can be, and will be alert to the non-neutral words or leading questions in other questionnaires, whether these are in newspaper opinion polls or in the more extensive and weighty work of the academic sociologist. Someone who has himself struggled with untidy and sporadically available documentation will be aware of the historian's temptation to cover up the blank patches with words. The student who has been, if only for a short time, a craftsman-academic, handling the raw materials of history, sociology, geology or ecology, will inevitably see the structure of another craftsman's work more clearly than he would had he remained only an onlooker, however well informed.

Extra demands

These are joys for the students who survive the course. Undoubtedly many students find project work altogether too demanding, and once they discover what is involved, may drop out altogether. Work on a project cannot be tidily confined to two hours in one place once a week. It makes demands on time and money which many students will feel they cannot meet. A group investigating the recent past of their own geographically small area, at present the most simple and commonly undertaken project, will still find that plenty of time is needed for the leisurely interviews with old people with long memories who can recall the tea parties, the workhouse, the scares over smallpox, the old tyrant at the big house – all the living detail which will bring a local history alive. Money may be needed for travelling, for buying reference books, for postage, for telephone calls. Some departments or LEAs may not be generous enough to supply this kind of support, so that it may fall to students to pay these perhaps quite sizeable expenses themselves. The work itself, fascinating at the outset or in its larger aspects, will undoubtedly have a tedious and dreary side when time is absorbed by ploughing through census returns or coding questionnaires for the computer, when real results seem far away.

In a group working well, the growing sense of fellowship and group feeling produced by working towards a common goal will usually be sufficiently strong to carry students over the difficult patch where academic or personal energies seem to be flagging. In other groups this may be the moment when the whole project seems endangered and the teacher must perform some sort of inspirational rescue job.

The teacher's problems

Here, as throughout the work, the teacher's role is a vital, delicate and exhausting one. He has most certainly abdicated from any pedagogic dominance. In his occasional lectures given to fill in background or to introduce a new part of the project, he will be listened to respectfully, possibly with more attention but certainly with more critical scrutiny than before; he will have become in a noticeable way the servant of the group rather than its master. A group working on a project will quickly gain confidence from close familiarity with the raw material; the sum of their local knowledge will be greater, more intimate usually, than that of the teacher, however well informed he keeps himself of work in hand.

He must know the abilities of his students and be aware of their friendships and antipathies. People work best when encouraged to work with their friends. A tutor who is ignorant of the particular bonds between students, or who deliberately and despotically sets out to destroy old bonds and create new ones, will surely wreck the project or weaken its effectiveness. Similarly there is no point in attempting to force students to undertake work which seems to them at first grandiose or alarming. People who are frightened by the idea of tasks such as conducting interviews or coping with medieval documents should not be jollied or shamed into attempting them; instead the teacher should keep the channels of opportunity open, so that if and when the less confident students change their minds it is possible for them to do so at any time without loss of face. The teacher should in any case try to prevent the growth of the situation seen in some project groups where some tasks come to seem humble and some important. Working in pairs rather than individually is one way round this problem, and it also overcomes the initial anxiety some students may feel that they are not capable of doing well whatever job they have been allotted. With someone else to share the responsibility, the possibility of letting the group down or failing the teacher in some way does not seem so frightening.

The majority of projects so far produced by groups both in Britain and in the United States have been of a sociological, archaeological or historical kind, and have involved groups in work lasting at least one and frequently three or more years. These protracted time-scales and apparently limited subject-areas have been a disincentive to teachers in other subjects and with less time at their disposal. There is, however, no reason why more modest work could not be attempted, some of it of an individual sort within a group, some of it short-term work for the whole group. Some starts have already been made. Two members of a WEA group studying local dialects in Staffordshire produced a pamphlet on children's rhymes, games and jokes; a group studying natural history who began with lectures but who wanted to test their knowledge in practice used part of their spring and summer sessions to make a census of breeding birds in one town.

Possibilities in adult education

So far most of this work has been done by single classes under a university or WEA flag, but it could be undertaken equally often and with equal efficiency by local-authority classes, or by several classes working as a team with a number of tutors. A class working on car maintenance might well be involved at some time in a town-planning traffic survey, and might work together with a group studying architecture or sociology; a language class might make a feasibility study of a 'twinning' link between the town and a foreign city, working together with a local-history group; an industrial-relations class might engage on an examination of a local labour problem and draw in members of management training courses or classes studying economics and law.

The project itself need not necessarily be local or stereotyped in form. Some of the most striking work of this kind, admittedly done within the structure of full-time art education, has been produced by Albert Hunt at Bradford. Working with groups for a fortnight at a time his students have, for example, investigated the raid on Dresden; invented and then played children's games; invented a religion and then tried to convert people to it; researched the life of the murderer Christie; researched then rehearsed the details of the Cuban missile crisis; and explored themes such as incarceration. Some of these projects have been written up by students, some have been the basis of improvised theatre, in some the students felt that the experience was the sort where no formal end product was appropriate – the fortnight's work must simply be absorbed and pondered individually and left at that. Other kinds of adult education have so far been too timid and perhaps too surprised by this type of work to attempt to copy it, but it is the sort of bold and imaginative teaching situation which might well offer the kind of experiment which adult education has often sought but rarely found.

However, projects are not panaceas. There is no point in embarking on a survey if someone else has already produced a more than adequate one in the recent past. A project will no more inevitably save a dull class than it will engage the energies and attentions of a lively one. Projects are not miraculous teaching techniques to be produced out of a hat, but means to serve educational and possibly social ends, and to be employed therefore with proper caution and respect.

Chapter 9
Discussion

In the extracts below all the teachers and students quoted felt sure that 'discussion' accurately described what was going on in their classes:

After an hour and a quarter lecture from me we have a coffee break, then discussion. The class usually raises such pertinent points that lengthy answers are needed from me, so that it sometimes needs miniature lectures to give a satisfactory reply. The class is exhausting for this reason.

During discussion we are speaking to each other, exploring, exchanging views, learning from each other: tutor from students, students from tutor, students from students.

I dislike the discussion part of the class because some members (not me) always lose their tempers.

In my dressmaking class we often have informal discussions, in small groups like ordinary conversation on materials, costs, fashion, design. Dressmaking cannot be cut off from questions of good taste, aesthetic judgement and design.

He is a very good teacher and we have a lot of interesting discussions, but he does love us to come round to his point of view!

In discussion I believe in quick-fire question-and-answer technique. It keeps them on their toes.

I encourage them to be frank. The content of the course (psychology) is less important than the business of learning to work as a group and getting to know yourself. I say virtually nothing. They do all the talking.

Clearly there are wide variations in the activities of these classes. One teacher seems to talk all the time, another says 'virtually nothing'; the atmosphere of the discussion in one class is mild and conversational, in another it is fierce and argumentative, in yet another personal and intense. Most important of all, the extracts show something of the fundamental divergences of opinion about the purpose and value of the discussion process itself, a divergence often concealed by the umbrella of a word such as 'discussion', which has such vague and comfortable associations.

Some teachers clearly believe that the point of a discussion is to change the attitudes of the class, usually in the direction of the teacher's views on a particular issue. Others believe in discussion because students enjoy it and they think there should be parts of a class which students enjoy. Others again are never quite sure why they do it, but feel that somehow it must be a good thing. With this theoretical vagueness 'discussion' as it is usually applied can mean anything from a few questions tossed to a class at the end of a gruelling lecture session to a solemn ninety minutes given over entirely to something very near group therapy.

What is 'discussion'?

Group therapy has its value, so does a question and answer session, so does a debate, but none of these processes is authentic discussion. Dividing discussions into good and bad, sheep and goats, can be narrowing, but a rough definition of real as opposed to imitation discussion might be that it is a situation where students and teacher can and do make an open, equal and personal response to a book, a philosophical theory, an industrial-relations problem, a current fashion in dress, a social trend, or anything else which needs interpretation to take it beyond a factual statement. The implications of this sort of discussion are that in controversial personal, social and academic areas, the student as an adult member of society has as much right to articulate and expect respect for his point of view as the teacher.

Discussion defined in this way is a very different thing from what passes for discussion in most adult classes. It becomes a time when the teacher shows the class that he has abandoned his teaching role as such, that he is encouraging what R. W. K. Paterson describes as a 'common search for meanings. For two people to "discuss" some piece of news is for them to ask each other "What does it mean?" ' *

*R. W. K. Paterson, 'The concept of discussion,' *Studies in Adult Education*, vol. 2, no. 1, 1970.

This search for meanings is frequently given the educational justification that it consolidates knowledge, improves the social atmosphere of the group, allows people to test themselves, and so on, but in fact discussion is in itself a supremely valuable process, whether it is used for a few minutes in a dressmaking class or whether it becomes the main method of learning in a sociology class. To quote Paterson again:

To unfold the meaning of a poem by discovering oneself and one's world in the face of a poem, to experience the sympathetic, critical, understanding, puzzled, consenting and demurring responses of others similarly occupied, and to respond in turn to their self-disclosures and self-commitments – to do all this is surely to engage in a type of activity which is educationally intimate.

The teacher's use of authority

Many teachers would claim that they already have the sort of respect for their students which makes the discussions in their classrooms as free as it is possible to make them. However, teachers too easily assume the tremendous mantle of authority their profession has acquired from teaching children. Furthermore, many of them are unaware of how much influence they have with their classes and of how easily this influence can be exerted affectionately as well as brusquely. It is often as easy for the adult teacher to do this as it is for the schoolteacher, given the diffidence of an inexperienced adult student, or of a new class of students anxious not to declare themselves too soon:

I thought I'd let other people do all the talking. I felt too ignorant to open my mouth.

I knew I'd blush if I spoke, so I never spoke.

Discussion is all right for those who are well informed. Other people always seem to know so much more than me.

Classroom discussions, closely analysed, will often reveal how frequently teachers capitalize on their traditional authority and on the humble feelings of their students. As a result, many discussions in adult education are far from free or equal, because the teacher, often quite unconsciously, guides, manipulates and dominates proceedings where it is inappropriate for him to do so.

For instance, he may feel obliged to follow every comment from a student with a longer one of his own. Students will hardly ever talk to other students under this system, the communication may be brisk and lively, but it will be in several sets of two-way traffic, student to teacher, teacher to student. An analysis of this sort of discussion usually reveals that the tutor talks almost all the time.

It is hard discipline for a teacher to keep his mouth shut, to listen, and to show signs of listening instead of talking. Most teachers are good at talking and especially enjoy talking about their subject. Not talking can be most exquisite agony, as any experienced teacher will know.

Some teachers may encourage student contributions, but may set up what has accurately been diagnosed as a 'guessing-game'. The game is played so that the student can hardly ever win, as in this brief transcript from a class comparing two poems by Wordsworth. The atmosphere of the class was entirely friendly and informal.

TUTOR: Well now, you've all read the second poem again, I hope. (*Murmurs of agreement.*) One thing that struck me, one thing I'm wondering, did you see any striking difference between this poem and the last one we read.

STUDENT 1: It's longer! (*Laughter and pause.*)

TUTOR: Well . . . yes!

STUDENT 2: Is it that this poem is somehow more . . . well, not so personal, it seems to have less of Wordsworth himself in it?

TUTOR: Yes. But I was thinking of something else.

STUDENT 3: The language is not so rich? Fewer metaphors?

TUTOR: Yes, a good point. That's certainly true. We'll look at that later. Anyone got any more ideas?

STUDENT 1: I don't like it! (*Laughter.*)

TUTOR: Any more bright ideas? (*Pause.*) Well, what I was thinking was that this poem is much more in the ballad vein, isn't it? It's reminiscent of the old simple Scottish ballads – can anyone tell us what a ballad is?

The teacher's views

In this situation the teacher has said in effect to the class, 'Now guess what I've got in mind?' The trouble is that there may be dozens of legitimate points of comparison between two poems, any one of which he may have in mind. The class plays along for a while, then says or signifies by silence the equivalent of 'I give up', after which the teacher announces the 'answer'. Not only does this sort of technique suggest to a class that there is only one acceptable and right major point of comparison, it also suggests that responses to a poem have to be tackled in a particular order (the suggestion about metaphor was pushed aside for 'later'), and that it is the response the teacher himself has in mind which is the most important one. Such a discussion technique ignores the possibility that students themselves can and should make fresh and direct contributions of a quality which would surprise a teacher who thinks his are the only interpretations which count.

Guessing-games develop out of a confusion in the teacher's mind between real discussion and question and answer. There are subjects – mathematics, for instance – where it might be legitimate for a teacher to say something like 'Can anyone tell me what the square root of forty-four is?' because there is only one possible answer. It is surprising how few such subjects are, and at what a low factual and academic level they have to function for it to be possible to deal with them in so summary a fashion.

Teachers may press their own views in other, more subtle ways. They may reward someone who offers a view agreeing with their own by nodding vigorously or by saying, 'Yes, a good point', or by following it up with some forceful elaboration of their own. They may frown doubtfully at a student giving an opposite opinion, or imply by the coolness of their nod on receiving the comment that only courtesy prevents them saying that such a comment was ridiculous, or inappropriate. They may initiate the discussion and prod it along with leading questions, as in this sociology class (again the atmosphere of this particular class was noticeably relaxed and uninhibited):

TUTOR: Don't you think society is still rather hard on unmarried mums?

STUDENT 1: Well, no, it's much easier now for a girl to keep her baby, isn't it?

TUTOR: But don't we all disapprove secretly of someone breaking the code?

STUDENT 2: The girl gets all the blame.

A.L.—9

STUDENT 3: It's the child that suffers.

STUDENT 4: There's a girl living near us with a baby and people avoid her, I think they feel embarrassed by her.

TUTOR: Do you talk to her?

STUDENT 4: Well – now and again, but I don't know her very well. She keeps herself to herself.

TUTOR: Why do you think this is? Is it because society punishes deviants? Isn't it that we all feel threatened by someone who has chosen not to conform?

STUDENT 2: Yes.

STUDENT 3: That's true.

The phrasing of the teacher's initial question has given the class a clue either to his own view, or to what he interprets as the common view of a familiar social problem. It may be that the teacher can offer the class evidence on how 'society' views unmarried mothers – surveys, novels, articles – but he notably does not do this. He quickly tries to encourage the group to confess to prejudice themselves, and seizes on a personal anecdote told by one student as the occasion to drive home his point by virtually accusing the student who told it of prejudice herself. In such discussion the teacher gives it a gloss of freedom, but in fact he is seeking for confirmation of his own view and moral standpoint (and in the extract quoted, eventually wins it superficially) almost as firmly as the teacher in the guessing-game.

The information and sources a tutor uses for discussion may easily be chosen to support his own view. The group here is usually at the mercy of the teacher unless they are lucky enough or enterprising enough to discover the bias for themselves:

Between school and university I took a year's voluntary job, but to keep my hand in I thought I'd go to an extra-mural class in my own subject – history. It appealed to me because it was advertised as a course using original documents of the period, with lots of opportunities for discussion. It was very interesting and the lecturer was superb – a real enthusiast. I only discovered how incredibly partisan his view of the period was when in my third year at university I realized how his enthusiasm for one school of thought had totally affected the documents he gave us and the evidence we used for our discussions. He was quite unaware of what he had done, I'm sure.

The dangers of planning

Some teachers attempt to control a discussion by drawing up detailed plans for it in advance. Control can become manipulation where a teacher also tries to anticipate the *content* of the students' answers. It is fair enough for a teacher to have a rough plan in mind and to have at hand the materials and information needed to explore the likely ramifications of the three or four questions any one class could be expected to explore in a few hours, but he should always be prepared to abandon this plan if the interest of the class points clearly in another direction. What seems a red herring to a tutor may well be an absorbing topic to his students. Each red herring should be judged on its merits by other students as well as the teacher. It certainly seems a mistake for a teacher to have too many rigid expectations about the length, content and likely conclusions of a discussion. In opening up discussion a teacher is offering the class something free, floating and unpredictable. It is not possible to chart too closely in advance the form the discussion should take, for the essence of a valuable discussion is the unexpectedness and originality of the new territory which should constantly be explored. It is only when the students can see that the teacher is genuinely offering them opportunities to speculate, think and interpret that new ideas will flourish.

A good discussion inevitably exposes the ambiguities and complexities of a topic. Many teachers, searching for a way to find a framework for their students that will hold widely diverging views, will attempt to impose a 'conclusion' on the discussion which can easily be a false representation of what has been said:

It puzzled me at first, but I never recognized his summaries as accounts of what we had all said. After a bit I realized that the summary represented (a) his own opinion, (b) what he wished we had said. I think we must have disappointed him by not being such a bright class as he'd hoped. We certainly weren't up to his standards.

Paterson makes the same point from an educationist's view:

One inevitably wonders how many ... counterfeit discussions are staged in adult classes by tutors whose confidence in their own preferred views disables them from taking the views of their students with the utmost seriousness required of all participants in the authentic educational dialogue. I am referring less to the assertive and dogmatic tutor than to the kind of tutor who unobtrusively and skilfully synthesizes the various discussion contributions of his students, by judicious selection and emphasis, into a neatly structured and rounded proposition or body of propositions, which are then represented as the 'conclusions' of the 'class discussion', although they have in fact been evolved by the tutor who has ingeniously utilized the discussion, always more or less under his discreet control, as an educational device for arranging precisely this body of propositions, deemed by him to be of some importance to his students at this stage of their classwork. The teaching skill exercised by such a tutor may be of a very high order, and the results gained may be of great educational value. To the extent that his students believe themselves to be participating in a genuinely open-ended dialogue, however, they are being misled; and to the extent that he believes himself to be 'conducting a discussion', he is misleading himself.*

It is, of course, the teacher's job to present a discussion to a group in such a way that members can see they have learnt from it, but it seems a false way to set about this delicate task by using phrases such as 'Well, I think we're all agreed that . . .' or 'Everyone seems to have come to the conclusion that . . .'. It is highly unlikely that all students are of one mind on any topic worth extended discussion, and it is the teacher's task to see that a false consensus does not emerge. He should encourage and maintain divergent views, even where they conflict sharply with his own. As Albert Mansbridge said: 'The class is not intended for the passing of resolutions, but is rather a means whereby all relevant facts and arguments may be looked at and turned over.'

Controversial issues

However, it is easier to look at and turn over some facts than others. On many of the issues which come up in adult classes, teachers as well as students may have such strong opinions that they find it hard to resist voicing them. Making an outburst is one thing, using their authority to deliver some final *coup de grâce* on the argument is another. Teachers who are too cool will

* Paterson, 'The concept of discussion', 1970.

be resented by their classes; teachers who are too heated may lose their respect:

I remember one discussion on race – a topic chosen by the group (young adults) where I sat back and let them get on with it. This was in Birmingham and there was a fair sprinkling of coloured students in the group. I was frankly appalled by the massive generalizations and contradictory assertions voiced by those who should have known better. All those terrible statements like – 'They take all the jobs' but 'live on national assistance'. Those hoary old apocryphal stories were trotted out – 'I know a man who lives next door to them – and they pee in the back garden.' All that sort of thing. Perhaps what annoyed me most was their attitude towards the coloured students there, they were so insensitive even when one – a popular West Indian student – got up and left, obviously very upset.

Just before the end of the session I decided I could contain myself no longer and took charge. I rounded on them and told them if I were coloured I would feel like those in the Black Power movement – I would scream 'Burn, baby, burn' – I would feel my only hope was to destroy by physical means the white man's domination.

I am afraid they were horribly shocked by my outburst. It took a lot of time before our relationship returned to normal.

How can a teacher avoid uncomfortable situations like this? How does the teacher recognize and cope with his own bias but still use the discussion method? How can information and ideas of all sorts be presented to the group so that both discussing and learning take place?

One significant recent development in education has been the work of the Humanities Project of the Schools Council, which is aimed at adolescents but has important implications for adult education. The project has investigated ways of dealing with controversial topics through discussion rather than instruction, and has defined a controversial issue as

one which divides students, parents and teachers because it involves an element of value judgement which prevents the issue's being settled by evidence and experiment.

There may be consensus among students, parents and teachers at high levels of generality, an agreement, for example, that other things being equal, war is a bad thing. In practice this does not help the teacher, since effective discussion concentrates for much of the time on specific issues which are inevitably highly controversial. Should we have dropped the bomb on Hiroshima? Were the two world wars justified? Should the Americans be in Vietnam? *

Laurence Stenhouse, the Project Director, has come to the conclusion that the only tenable position for a teacher wishing to introduce such important and controversial topics in a classroom is to adopt a 'value-neutral' position. The 'value-neutral' teacher is aware of his own bias, but 'as students often put it, the teacher may agree not to take sides in their discussion'. Since the teacher who adopts this stance can no longer be the sole source of information, the project has developed and published a battery of 'evidence' – by which it means any relevant poetry, drama, photographs, tapes, films – around major themes such as War or the Family which become the centre of a discussion in which the teacher acts as procedural guide but not moral mentor.

The project itself is controversial. The methods it advocates involve radical changes in a teacher's role, and seem to many teachers to rob them of prized chances to give advice to vulnerable adolescents. Management of the plethora of resources can be tricky both from a logical and a moral point of view, since the teacher may continue to push his own opinion through the 'evidence' he offers the group. Management of the students can be exhausting, the authority of the teacher, and his relationships within the class and the school, change drastically towards a more democratic and egalitarian situation to which many teachers find it hard to adjust.

Nevertheless, the teaching strategy has been shown to work, and its principles might well be applied as successfully in adult education, where there is a healthy tradition of discussion in classes and where the procedures of the project might well be valuably extended to more factual subjects.

Investment of emotion

Emotion comes even into judging facts and superficially more neutral scientific subjects, as was interestingly shown by M. L.

* Humanities Curriculum Project, 'The Humanities Project: an introduction', Schools Council and Nuffield Foundation, Heinemann, 1970.

Johnson Abercrombie in her work with medical students who, in one set of experimental free discussions (that is, with no academic direction from a teacher), were asked to compare two radiographs of a hand. The results showed how many unjustifiable assertions the students were inclined to make on sparse evidence, how frequently they saw what they expected to see, and how emotionally they would defend their conclusions:

The inferences the students had made were not arrived at as a result of a series of logical steps, but swiftly, almost unconsciously. The validity of the inferences was usually not inquired into, indeed the process was usually accompanied by a feeling of certainty of being right, and consequently the discussion of incompatible views sometimes became very heated. Frequently the correct inference had been made (as with the statement that A was a younger hand than B), and then discussion did not change the formulation of the end result, but only brought to light the processes involved in getting it.*

This concern with evidence, with logical processes, with the distinction between factual information and what can be deduced from it, is the educational end which discussion is superbly well equipped to fulfil. Abercrombie summarizes her aim in the course of unguided discussions as being 'to make it possible for the student to relinquish the security of thinking in well-defined given channels and to find a new kind of stability based on the recognition and acceptance of ambiguity, uncertainty and open choice'. This might well serve as an aim for most of the courses in adult education which use a discussion method as one of their tools.

The flow of resources

There are problems in instigating discussion which is as free and open as the sort described in this chapter. 'Free' group discussion is frequently denigrated as 'the pooling of ignorance', and it seems clear that if discussion is to be more than this, the group must have a constant flow of new information and ideas. Traditionally these have come from the teacher, but the teacher is at the mercy of his own bias, probably as much so in academic subjects as he

*M. L. Johnson Abercrombie, *The Anatomy of Judgement*, Hutchinson, 1960; Penguin, 1969.

is in matters of value judgements. In a course where there is no lecturing at all from the teacher and where the learning is done entirely through discussion, the teacher's role becomes more concentrated on the flow of resources, many of which might be digested outside the class time. For instance, some of the classes studying social psychology for an Open University preparatory course listened to the BBC radio programme, read a textbook, did correspondence course at home, and used the class time for watching a television programme and for discussion. In this way assimilation was tested, meaning and interpretations compared, difficulties talked out in a way that had nothing to do with a pooling of ignorance. A teacher who does not have the benefit of a ready-made 'multi-media' course can still construct one – at more time, trouble and cost, of course – by establishing his own collection of documents, tapes and photographs, to which he *and the group* are constantly adding. All discussion is demanding of a teacher, but the freer the discussion and the more nearly it approaches an open exchange of views of the Humanities Project type, the greater the skill demanded of the teacher.

Problems

Free discussion may solve some problems, but it undoubtedly creates others. For instance, some students are satisfied enough with a teacher who is willing to tell them what to think, and may be quite happy with the appearance and not the substance of discussion, simply because a substantial discussion in an educational setting may be unfamiliar as well as demanding. The only school experience of 'discussion' many people have may well be something close in spirit to the dismal process Charles Dickens satirized in *Hard Times* over a hundred years ago, when he set the first scene of his attack on the cold spirit of utilitarianism in Mr Gradgrind's school during a visit by a 'government officer' – perhaps an earlier, grimmer version of a modern HMI:

'Bitzer,' said Thomas Gradgrind. 'Your definition of a horse.'

'Quadruped. Graminivorous. Forty teeth, namely twenty-four grinders, four eye-teeth, and twelve incisive. Sheds coat in the spring; in marshy countries, sheds hoofs, too. Hoofs hard, but requiring to be shod with iron. Age known by marks in mouth.' Thus (and much more) Bitzer.

'Now girl number twenty,' said Mr Gradgrind. 'You know what a horse is.'

She curtsied again, and would have blushed deeper, if she could have blushed deeper than she had blushed all this time. Bitzer, after rapidly blinking at Thomas Gradgrind with both eyes at once, and so catching the light upon his quivering ends of lashes that they looked like the antennae of busy insects, put his knuckles to his freckled forehead and sat down again.

The third gentleman now stepped forth. A mighty man at cutting and drying, he was; a government officer; in his way (and in most other people's too), a professed pugilist; always in training, always with a system to force down the general throat like a bolus, always to be heard of at the bar of his little Public-office, ready to fight. All England. To continue in fistic phraseology, he had a genius for coming up to the scratch, wherever and whatever it was, and proving himself an ugly customer. He would go in and damage any subject whatever with his right, follow up with his left, stop, exchange, counter, bore his opponent (he always fought All England) to the ropes, and fall upon him neatly. He was certain to knock the wind out of common-sense, and render that unlucky adversary deaf to the call of time. And he had it in charge from high authority to bring about the great Public-office Millenium, when Commissioners should reign upon earth.

'Very well,' said this gentleman, briskly smiling, and folding his arms. 'That's a horse. Now, let me ask you girls and boys, would you paper a room with representations of horses?'

After a pause, one half of the children cried in chorus, 'Yes, sir!' Upon which the other half, seeing in the gentleman's face that Yes was wrong, cried out in chorus, 'No, sir!' – as the custom is, in these examinations.

'Of course, No. Why wouldn't you?'

A pause. One corpulent slow boy, with a wheezy manner of breathing, ventured the answer, Because he wouldn't paper a room at all, but would paint it.

'You *must* paper it,' said Thomas Gradgrind, 'whether you like it or not. Don't tell *us* you wouldn't paper it. What do you mean, boy?'

'I'll explain to you, then,' said the gentleman, after another and a dismal pause, 'why you wouldn't paper a room with representations of horses. Do you ever see horses walking up and down the sides of rooms in reality – in fact? Do you?'

'Yes, sir!' from one half. 'No, sir!' from the other.

'Of course no,' said the gentleman, with an indignant look at the wrong half. 'Why, then, you are not to see anywhere, what you don't see in fact; you are not to have anywhere, what you don't have in fact. What is called Taste, is only another name for Fact.'

Students accustomed to a teacher who seems omniscient may take time to find the courage to speak freely in a class, or to believe that their contributions really are being taken seriously. Indeed, after a while when it is clear that they are being listened to with scrupulous attention by teacher and other students, this may in itself be alarming. A student who can throw in a frivolous comment in a discussion dominated by the teacher may be over-whelmed by the responsibility of speaking in a serious discussion where the emphasis is on the students.

Others may resent a teacher who does not take a dominant role, and may attack the teacher by saying something like 'You're the teacher, you've studied the subject longer than we have. Why don't you tell us?' This situation sometimes develops in a class where the teacher is clearly keeping something up his sleeve, and deceiving the class about his own opinions or holding back useful knowledge. I once watched a teacher, who believed in never under any circumstances giving his own view, attacked by an exasperated class after he had answered perhaps the tenth direct question from one of his students with 'I don't know, what do you think?' He received the tart and well-deserved response 'But you *do* know and you ought to tell us.'

Discussion can often seem ragged and inconclusive, especially to students used to learning one 'right' answer. These students may find the ambiguity of a discussion too trying, and many others will feel that 'just talking' is a waste of time. These students might share Professor Max Beloff's view that 'the don teaches the undergraduate for the same reason that the master teaches the boy: he knows more', a view that denies the possibility that students can and frequently do surpasss the master and learn from each other, especially when opportunities are made for them to do so and the skills of discussion are learnt by students as well as practised by the teacher. Nevertheless, many discussions can seem time-wasting, and with adult classes making heavy reliance on the discussion process it is essential to try various ways of consolidating it with note-taking, written work based on the discussion, or personal research undertaken as a result of points made during it, as well as progress reports, or discussions on the discussions.

This kind of work can also be the occasion for correcting the mistakes and factual errors inevitably made by students in the course of discussion. Mistakes the teacher diagnoses as 'dangerous' can properly be corrected in the classroom, but the responsibility for doing this need not always be the teacher's. Usually there are plenty of students as capable of making the correction as the teacher. Otherwise, a quiet word after the class or before the next one is usually more effective than a public reproof.

Conflict and argument

The teacher must remain ultimately responsible for the mood and atmosphere of his class. Hectic, fevered discussion can arouse a priceless interest and excitement in a topic, and it does no harm to bring disputes into the open. Sometimes, however, discussions become so heated and the participants so involved that they become angry. Discussion can then be confused with argument, with one 'side' of a class ranged implacably against the other. The point of the discussion turns away from the educational objective of exchanging opinions, listening to and learning from other people, and turns instead into a battle where one side has to concede defeat and lose face:

Every time the class met, although it was nineteenth-century social and political history we were discussing, the discussion always got round to politics today. We all knew Mr — was a keen Labour man because he was on the council. He didn't say it himself, but I felt he used to encourage one or two others to argue it out. Sometimes it got nasty and there would be name-calling, etc. On one occasion it was serious and one of his opponents was so angry he refused to come to the pub afterwards. I felt the teacher ought to have stopped it but it was hard to see what more she could have done other than try to keep the peace a bit better.

In a situation like this education has flown out of the window. People who are encouraged to state extreme views with such vigour are well on the way to finding it impossible to listen to anyone else. Having committed themselves vehemently and publicly to one view, it becomes difficult to retract or to explore the possibility that other people may have a view which is equally valid. The point of discussion should not be to establish a majority view, or even any one range of views, but to develop understanding, to learn how to make up one's mind, how to assess evidence, how to formulate conclusions. The conclusion itself may well be an irrelevance. A teacher who sees argument rather than discussion developing will do well to use his authority to cool the atmosphere with a joke or an invitation to examine some evidence, or to ask some other student to contribute.

It may be that some teachers are glad to see arguments develop because teachers tend to evaluate the discussions in their classrooms in terms of how 'stimulating' or 'lively' they are. Not all discussions need to be noisy or obviously vigorous to be educationally valuable. A good discussion may be quiet, apparently low key, with a lot of thoughtful silences. Teachers are often afraid of silence and leap in to fill any pause that looks like becoming an embarrassment, perhaps because long silences have connections with social embarrassment. A class which has established that a pause can continue until someone is ready to fill it with a considered comment may well produce more measured and telling points than the hastier, superficial sparkle of a lively, non-stop discussion.

Individual contributions

Nevertheless, in a good discussion most members of a group will feel willing and able to speak when appropriate. Many of the anxieties of teachers and the grumbles of students concern the numbers of people participating in any one discussion. Three typical comments illustrate familiar situations:

A lot of the people there had been going to WEA classes for years. They knew each other and they knew the tutor, so no one else got a look in.

My *bête noire* was a man who would always try to prove me wrong at great length. He was being forced by his union to attend, so he always felt he had to show he already knew everything that I was teaching. He tried to dominate every discussion.

I always thought our discussions were good, but one evening for interest, I counted up the number who had said something. I was horrified to discover that only six out of sixteen had said anything.

Even in a group where everybody contributes at some time, there will always be some who talk more than others. This can be a cause for concern if those who talk most are preventing other people from joining in, or are seeming to waste the group's time with rambling anecdotes, with harangues, or simply with information too difficult for the rest of the group to understand. Adult groups often contain one member who is more knowledgeable than the rest. It is tempting for a teacher to engage one prominent student in discussion – sometimes simply out of pleasure in talking, sometimes because of a cowardly wish to placate a student who might otherwise become bored and restless. The short-term solution is to let him get on with it, but a teacher who habitually allows one student to dominate a class is only storing up trouble for the future. It is unfair to other students, who eventually become irritated and fidgety and may leave the class rather than sit through more sessions of a dialogue between a teacher and an apparently favoured student.

It is better instead for a tutor to encourage students to develop self-criticism about the quality and length of their own contributions. The teacher can set the pace by inviting the group to evaluate each other's contributions: 'Does any one have a comment on that?' or 'What do other people think?' In a class where this capacity has been encouraged, students are often able to interrupt a lengthy contribution either with challenges and questions, with comments of their own or, as I saw once in a philosophy class, simply with a good-humoured, 'You've had three minutes by my watch, time to let someone else in now!'

Nevertheless, dominant members of groups are often able and energetic people, whose initiative and enthusiasm can be valuable to the rest of the group, either in the ideas they contribute to general discussion, or in the extra research, short lectures and special assignments they may occasionally be encouraged to undertake. A careful balance must clearly be kept between letting them tyrannize a group on the one hand, and letting them waste their talents on the other. Teachers are sometimes advised to speak privately after the class to an over-talkative student, asking him to talk less. This can sometimes be effective and may be the appropriate thing to do, but it is a procedure which runs the risk of seeming impertinent or else suggesting a conspiracy between the teacher and his specially clever student, both of whom agree to patronize the less fortunate slower people. The class itself is always a better vehicle for carrying out such operations.

Silent members of a class, or people who speak only rarely in a discussion, can present problems to a teacher who does not want to bully people into speaking but who wants to see everyone make some sort of contribution. People who do not speak can be silent as a way of showing disapproval of what the rest of the group are saying; they can be silent out of shyness or diffidence or laziness; silent because although they would like to speak, conditions never seem right for them to take the plunge; or simply silent because they prefer to listen to other people rather than talk themselves.

Each case must be judged on its merits. There is no evidence to equate participation in discussion with learning, and if people prefer to be silent it could be an impertinence to try forcing them to speak. Attempting to draw out a shy student by addressing direct questions to him may face him with an excruciating ordeal and may, in any case, fail to produce a response. I remember a student in one of my classes who simply stonewalled this attempt to be helpful by shaking her head silently and staring down at the desk. With other students it may provide them with just the opening they have been waiting for, but it is usually more successful if more vaguely directed than at an individual – 'Some of you have special knowledge of —. Would any of you like to say something on this?' Again, the rest of the group can be encouraged to look to each other for contributions, to get to know who has particular knowledge of or unusual opinions on some issue, and can therefore be expected to say something valuable.

When a shy or less dominant member does make a brief contribution to a discussion, it is often helpful if the teacher can rein in the discussion at that point to ask the student for further elaboration – 'It might be interesting if you expanded that point.' Alternatively, a tutor can suggest a general pause in the discussion by saying something like, 'We seem to have covered a lot of ground rather quickly. Can we stop to think for a moment?'

Focusing the discussion at one stage like this is often a useful way of allowing slower thinkers to catch up and speak if they want to. There may be opportunities to do the same thing at the beginning and end of a discussion. I have seen some tutors encourage silent students to speak at these points by saying, 'We left a lot unsaid at our last session. Is there anyone who would like to add anything now?' or 'Would anyone like the last word?' Such invitations have, of course, to be followed by a generous pause otherwise they might just as well not be made.

Problems of over-dominant and too-silent members can often be solved by splitting the group into smaller groups for some part of the class time:

We start off as one group – about fifteen of us – going over the week's written work, looking at a new poem or chapter. After coffee we divide into however many groups can be divided by three or four. Each group has a question written on a piece of paper. All the questions are closely related but different, and based on the topic we discussed before coffee. This takes twenty minutes, strictly timed. We then report back, compare questions, and have what is usually a most useful general discussion to finish off. With this system everybody who wants to can speak, and everyone is obliged to give really close attention to the text.

There are twenty-five students, two tutors. We watch the television programme together, discuss it for ten minutes, then split. People who never speak in the large group normally say quite a lot in the smaller one.

It is not unusual for the first five minutes of the discussion to be the slowest and the most difficult to manage, and the part of the process that teachers most dread. The best ways of encouraging discussion seem to be to ask students to prepare for it by thinking, reading and writing, to reassure them that silence does not matter, to make it clear that the teacher really has withdrawn from his role of pedagogue by saying 'Would anyone like to comment?' or some such phrase *and no more*. Most importantly the teacher must provide the group with an initial stimulus as emotionally gripping, or as intellectually intriguing and as complex as possible. This could be a lecture, a dramatic reading, a tape, a television or radio programme, a film, a case study or simulation, or anything else which demands an immediate response. Film and television are perhaps particularly useful in loosening tongues, as many people are used to discussing them informally without the strain that may be associated with academic discussion of a poem or book.

The teacher's role in discussion

The teacher's role in an authentic discussion is, then, a taxing one. He must first of all make sure that the students understand and share a common view of what discussion is by inviting them at the outset to discuss the discussion process, and by making it clear that his own role will be that of impartial chairman rather than active teacher, of careful listener rather than frequent speaker. He must be ready to clarify issues so that groups understand what they are discussing, and why. He must be ready to relate the issues of one discussion to issues raised and explored on previous occasions. He must see that the group eschews personal attacks and violent sarcasm, as well as dull restatement of old prejudices. He must encourage and protect minority views. He should make sure that students learn to distinguish between fact and opinion, and be ready to feed in the resources which could supply facts and opinions giving an opposite, even an unpopular view. He must set the linguistic tone by using language everyone can understand, he must make sure that opportunities are kept open so that people who want to speak can speak, he must encourage the art of listening as well as talking.

The paragon who can do all this, and who can at the same time train his group to take over these functions too, is offering his class a chance to learn in a unique way, by measuring minds and experiences with other people on equal terms.

The philosophical and democratic case for discussion, as well as by implication its educational justification, has never been made so powerfully as by John Stuart Mill in *On Liberty*; a case which can still serve as a model to any adult tutor today:

There must be discussion, to show how experience is to be interpreted. Wrong opinions and practices gradually yield to fact and argument; but facts and arguments, to produce any effect on the mind, must be brought before it. Very few facts are able to tell their own story, without comments to bring out their meaning. The whole strength and value, then, of human judgement, depending on the one property, that it can be set right when it is wrong, is that reliance can be placed on it only when the means of setting it to right are kept constantly at hand. In the case of any person whose judgement is really deserving of confidence, how has it become so? Because he has kept his mind open to criticism of his opinions and conduct. Because it has been his practice to listen to all that could be said against him; to profit by as much of it as was just, and expound to himself, and upon occasion to others, the fallacy of what was fallacious. Because he has felt, that the only way in which a human being can make some approach to knowing the whole of a subject, is by hearing what can be said about it by persons of every variety of opinion, and studying all modes in which it can be looked at by every character of mind. No wise man ever acquired his wisdom in any mode but this; nor is it in the nature of human intellect to become wise in any other manner.

Appendix:
Help from Outside

Many teachers of adults work in total isolation from one another. They earn insultingly small amounts of money. They teach in wildly unsuitable rooms. They have virtually no special training. The petty frustrations of their teaching environments can often seem overwhelming when it is combined with inexperience and lack of readily available advice:

Problems of a new teacher: primarily lack of accumulated material – nothing to fall back on. For every class one has to prepare it totally. All subjects must produce special problems – my dancing class was the most time-consuming. I had originally wanted to eliminate boring exercises, but was reduced to using them for half the class just because I had not the time nor inclination to think up creative dance steps for a two-hour stretch.

Other major problems: lack of facilities, bad and unsuitable rooms, no music library, no tape recorder, etc. In my experimental acting class we have a room where the acoustics are so bad nobody understands what anyone is saying, and where the furniture consists of kindergarten desks and chairs. For the dancing class we have a gym, a central assembly hall where people are constantly passing through (particularly a hooting, whistling football training class!).

Other grouses: inefficiency and lack of interest on the part of the principal; not enough money to encourage me to work in my own time, no expenses, and expecting hours of unpaid overtime for things like rehearsals.

I had to take the shop-stewards' course in the works canteen because there wasn't anywhere else we could have heard each other speak. It wasn't very suitable, mainly because there were always about thirty people there drinking, etc. and they would make 'funny' remarks about us all the way through.

Added to these familiar and irksome difficulties, there seems to be in some kinds of adult education a crushing, time-consuming load of paper work resulting in plain mystification or else trifling dishonesty:

We all knew the class had to keep up to eight on the register or else close, but even when we got down to five regulars he'd mark in eight or nine present saying 'I expect the others will be along later.'

I didn't know what I was supposed to do with the registers at the end of term, so I just tore them up. There was a terrible fuss when this was discovered, but the principal gave me some blank ones and told me to fill them as best I could 'from memory' – i.e. make them up.

I can't think of any more tedious part of the job than adding up hours and students at the end of term. It takes me literally days because I can never get my registers to balance.

This chapter is about some of the ways the teacher of adults can find advice and information on some of his major problems: his isolation, his need for training, and for resources.

Isolation

Even in industry the teacher of adults may feel isolated and lonely. His appointment may have been a sop to the training boards, and he may find himself doing little teaching but spending most of his time working as an unrecognized assistant to the personnel manager. In companies with large training schools the training officer's function is usually at least clearly defined; nevertheless some of the firm's reluctant adherence to the provisions of the Industrial Training Act, especially to its letter rather than its spirit, may rub off on the training officer, who may feel set apart both from his immediate colleagues and from education and training in general.

In voluntary adult education the situation is even worse. Apart from the small but growing number of full-time teachers interested in making adult education their career, there is a great army of part-timers, many of whom scuttle once a week for two hours into their university extra-mural departments, evening institute or adult centres, snatch a register, take their classes, and disappear home again with all possible speed. These teachers may not know the name of a single colleague; they may not even be aware that there are other teachers with exactly parallel classes on other nights of the week. The fault lies with both sides: with the teachers for being too timid, for accepting the status quo as inevitable, or for taking their work too lightly; with the organizers in not taking more positive steps to encourage greater professionalism and sense of community among their staff.

Saddest of all, it is rare in adult education for teachers employed by the university extra-mural departments or the WEA to meet regularly with teachers employed by the local authorities (except where they happen to work in the same building). It is rarer still even at the highest professional level for people concerned with teaching adults in industry to meet people concerned with teaching adults in local-authority or university centres. They undoubtedly share more problems than divide them. Even so there is still in each type of adult education a strong residue of wilful narrowness, where teachers divide themselves by subject, by intellectual level and by institutions ('I teach Advanced Dressmaking, so I don't have anything in common with her because she teaches Beginners' Embroidery' or 'I work for the WEA and our teaching traditions are so different from everyone else's that there's not much point in discussion with them').

As far as industry is concerned there seems very little realization that industrial experience in teaching manual or intellectual skills has much to offer the teacher of skills in adult education, that other kinds of adult education might benefit from the application of know-how gained from industrial research into adult learning, or that training officers in industry might learn from the accumulated expertise of the universities and local authorities in teaching adults.

Remedying this situation is impossible for the individual teacher unless he by-passes his own organization and sets up a local working group. A more normal and effective way of breaking down the first barriers is to get to know other teachers working in the same subject, or on the same day. Apart from this, these are some of the other ways in which a teacher can mitigate the worst of his professional loneliness.

Advice from outside

Advice from people able to see the national picture is obtainable from four main sources. No one of them is able to advise on the entire field of adult education and industrial training. In theory the three industrial organizations only give advice to individual subscribers or to people whose organization are members (almost all largish organizations *would* belong).

The British Association for Commercial and Industrial Training (BACIE), 16 Park Crescent, London, W1N 4AP, is the only independent and voluntary organization specializing entirely in vocational training for commerce and industry. It draws its membership and support from training boards, industry, employers' associations, educational bodies and trade unions. In return it offers an information service and specialist library, and a training department which runs its own courses, several publications and regional groups. Journals: *BACIE News* seven times yearly, *BACIE Journal* four times yearly.

The *British Institute of Management* (BIM), Management House, Parker Street, London, W C2. The BIM is independent, non-political and non-profit-making, and is supported by government grant and by subscriptions from member organizations, which include government departments, trade unions and educational institutions. The Institute has a sophisticated information retrieval system, and is a national clearing-house for information on management and training practices.

The Industrial Training Service, 53 Victoria Street, London, SW1, is the practical advisory service sponsored by the Central Training Council (the body which coordinates all the industrial training boards) and the Department of Employment. The ITS will advise on training needs of particular firms, develop training schemes, help form group training schemes for several companies faced with similar problems. Initial surveys are made free of charge.

The National Institute of Adult Education, 35 Queen Anne Street, London, W1M OBL, offers the individual teacher an indispensable bird's-eye view of his profession. It is supported and financed by all the organizations providing adult education in England and Wales, and is the only centrally organized body dealing with information about adult education on a national and international basis. As such it is the clearing-house for information and a useful place to make preliminary inquiries on adult-educational problems. The Institute maintains a library, promotes conferences, undertakes occasional pieces of research, publishes two magazines (see p. 200), and a *Year Book of Adult*

Education, which is an invaluable source of names, addresses and information on all providers of adult education.

Conferences

Conferences range from brief social gatherings whose educational purpose can be only dimly perceived, to the high-powered week-long events where the custom is to make conference members *work* literally morning, noon and night. This latter type is greatly to be preferred, as there is still time for talking round the bar or in the lounges, where a lot of people would claim, the *real* work of conferences goes on. Either way, conferences are one easily available way of meeting other teachers from outside one's own immediate geographical and subject area. The cost, ridiculously small for LEA or DES events, ridiculously large for industrial ones, can usually be partially or wholly defrayed by grants from local authorities and training boards.

The least useful type of conference is the one where several hundred people are kept together all day for several days to listen to a succession of eminent lecturers who stop five minutes before the end of their one-and-a-half-hour sessions to ask for 'questions'. The most useful type of conference is the one where there are not more than sixty people and not less than thirty, where there are a few brief and stimulating lecture sessions from people who know when to stop talking, where papers and booklists are distributed in advance, and where a good deal of the conference time is spent by hard work in small groups.

Conference calendars are published by the National Institute of Adult Education, 35 Queen Anne St, London W1M OBL, and the Youth Service Information Centre, Humberstone Drive, Leicester.

No overall information is available on industrial-training conferences, but most of the main training and management journals (see p. 200) give a conference diary.

Help from above

Extra-mural directors, professors, principals, heads of training, managing directors are not the remote and lofty figures most teachers or training officers seem to fear they may be. On the contrary, they are usually responsive to pressure for meetings, discussions, or simply social gatherings where people in the same trade can meet and talk. Accommodation difficulties may make them more resistant to pressure for a permanent common-room and coffee bar for staff, but in the long run this is a more valuable facility than occasional meetings. One teacher alone asking for such privileges is fairly easily put down, several teachers who can present a well-argued case are harder to oppose.

Consumers' associations usually advise complaining customers to go straight to the man at the top. This sound advice applies to adult education too, except that it is courteous to let the deputies and deputy-deputies know what is going on.

Industrial training boards

Industrial training boards would be the natural place for a training officer to seek preliminary advice on training problems. There are now about thirty ITBs, many of them with regional officers able to give on-the-spot help. Information about the boards and addresses can be obtained from the Department of Employment, 8 St James's Square, London, SW1.

Inspectors

Inspectors are no longer to be regarded as fearful ogres whose job is to catch the teacher out. Today's inspector is much more likely to be concerned with helping the teacher, training him, and generally acting as a repository of experience and wisdom on which he hopes the teacher will call. Her Majesty's Inspectors (HMIs) are employed by the Department of Education and Science. A good deal of their time is spent visiting classes, arranging conferences, and acting as clearing-house on current trends in education. Names of HMIs based in particular areas can be obtained from Her Majesty's Inspectorate, Department of Education and Science, Curzon Street, London, W1. Some local authorities also employ inspectors with a special responsibility for adult education. Their function is much the same except that, unlike the HMI, they only visit classes run by the local authority.

Inspectors, national or local, are thin on the ground. The chances of the individual teacher being visited by an inspector are pretty remote. Better to contact him direct than to hope for a visit.

Most local authorities, even if they have no inspector specially for adult education, have an adult-education specialist on their staff. He may be called 'assistant education officer', 'further education officer' or 'adviser', but whatever his designation his job is to maintain an overall view of and responsibility for adult education in this borough or county. He is the person to complain to if representations to the principal fail on matters such as salary claims, unsuitable premises, or caretakers persistently too eager to lock the buildings on the stroke of nine o'clock.

Magazines and journals

Magazines and journals will keep teachers in touch with some of the developments in their profession. The general educational press (for example, *The Times Educational Supplement*) often has articles on adult education and industrial training; many of the providing bodies, training boards and professional associations publish their own journals (e.g. the *WEA News*, the *Technical Journal of the ATTI*). However the main national journals and magazines devoted exclusively to teaching adults are:

Adult Education, a bi-monthly journal with fairly long articles on trends, aims and methods in the profession, published by the National Institute of Adult Education.

Industrial Training International, a monthly magazine published by the Pergamon Press. Its emphasis is on training in industry, commerce and further education.

Industrial and Commercial Training, a monthly magazine for training officers, published by John Wellens Ltd, Guildborough, Northampton.

Studies in Adult Education, published by David & Charles, Newton Abbot, is the newest and most learned of the adult-education journals, containing long and thoughtful pieces on research and trends. The journal is sponsored by the Universities Council for Adult Education – the organization which discusses common policy for university extra-mural departments.

Teaching Adults, published four times a year by the National Institute of Adult Education, is an informal magazine with brief practical articles on teaching method.

Professional associations

Professional associations are weak in adult education since there is no body strong enough or attractive enough to draw in the majority of training officers or the majority of teachers, particularly the part-timers who are still largely neglected. Most of the existing organizations therefore, although continuing to do useful work by arranging for exchange of information on teaching policy and method, are unable to bring much pressure to bear on employers where conditions of work are concerned. There is no organization able to speak for adult tutors on a wide, numerically strong and genuinely non-sectarian basis. The organizations of most interest to teachers and training officers are a mixed bag of professional qualifying bodies, trade unions, and organizations which exist simply to promote the exchange of information:

Association of Tutors in Adult Education, 47 Acacia Avenue, Huyton, Lancashire. Branch secretaries work on a regional basis throughout the country. Most members work for university extra-mural departments or the WEA.

Association of Teachers in Technical Institutions, Hamilton House, Mabledon Place, London, WC1. A TUC affiliated union, most of whose members are teaching in technical colleges. Journal: *Technical Journal*.

Association for Adult Education, 28 Greenhayes Avenue, Banstead, Surrey. Caters mainly for people working full time in the adult-education service of the local authorities.

National Federation of Continuative Teachers' Associations, 44 Trinity Church Square, Trinity Street, London, SE1. Caters mainly for teachers of practical subjects in evening institutes.

Society of Industrial Tutors, 6 Brook Rise, Chigwell, Essex. A fairly new organization which attempts to bridge the gap between adult education and industry by drawing membership from teachers and training officers in universities, technical colleges, WEAs, trade unions, industry and commerce. The society arranges conferences.

Institution of Training Officers, 55 Station Road, Beaconsfield, Bucks. This is the only organization which caters exclusively for the industrial-training officer. No official entrance qualifications are required, but these may be introduced in the future. At present the ITO exists to exchange information and news on

training policy and practice. Journal: *Training Officer*.
Institute of Personnel Management, 5 Winsley Street, Oxford
Circus, London, W1, reflects the strong historical associations
between personnel and training. The Institute maintains regional
branches and local training groups. There are several membership
grades, depending on qualifications and experience. The Institute
offers an examination of pass-degree standard, an information
service, and also runs courses and conferences. Journals:
Personnel (monthly) and *IPM Digest*.

Training

There are still professors and principals in adult education who
do not bother to train their teachers, as they claim that teaching
adults is a matter of 'instinct' or being a 'born teacher'. Similarly,
in industry there are still instructors and training officers
appointed to train other people without themselves having had
any training at all.

New teachers are not generally under any illusions about their
need for training:

I went into my classroom knowing absolutely nothing about teaching. I was amazed that they should have offered me the job as I was
completely frank about my ignorance on teaching method. When
they said that didn't matter, I thought it was rather odd – surely it
should have mattered!

A day's training could have saved me weeks of unnecessary work
and worry.

We had a one-day conference before term started where I thought
'at last – some help on teaching', but it was all about registers and
enrolments.

Fortunately the need for a wide variety of training courses
goes hand in hand with the growing urge to make adult education a profession. There are not nearly enough training courses;
many of the existing courses still offer long-winded disquisitions
on 'The History of Adult Education', and rely entirely on passive
methods of learning. The principles of a good training course
are no different from those of any other good method of teach-

ing adults, and the more the course relies on active learning, group discussions, projects and the like the more effective it is likely to be.

Full-time one-year courses at postgraduate level or its equivalent are run by the universities in Manchester, Nottingham, Glasgow, Edinburgh and Liverpool. The places are usually filled by people who have already decided to make adult education their career and who are looking for a qualification which will help them find senior jobs.

Part-time courses of a similar kind are run by Manchester, Nottingham and Hull Universities. At a less elevated academic level, the City and Guilds offer two examinations for intending teachers, either full- or part-time: the Further Education Teachers' Certificate no. 394, and the FE Teachers' Advanced Certificate no. 395. Individual technical colleges often offer courses for these certificates, which usually involve two evenings' work a week. The length of time taken over the courses may vary locally, but it will not be less than 150 hours of instruction. Information on local courses can be obtained from the City and Guilds of London Institute, 76 Portland Place, London, W1N 4AA.

Sandwich courses (where the tutor alternates a few weeks' attendance at a course with a few weeks at work) are more common in industry than in adult education. However, Nottingham University's course is available in sandwich form. This university also runs a sandwich course for part-time teachers of dress, design and allied crafts at the Loughborough College of Art and Design.

Short courses of an *ad hoc* kind are frequently arranged by the Department of Education and Science, by local authorities, by the Regional Councils for Further Education, and by individual centres and colleges.

The choice for training officers is both more and less wide. There are fewer long diploma-type courses (though more are proposed), many more short courses on specialized topics. The situation is confused by the presence of a number of commercially operated firms as well as non-profit-making voluntary bodies offering training-officer training. A list of courses can be obtained from the BACIE. BACIE do not themselves assess courses, but the British Institute of Management Education Information Unit and the De la Rue Index (PO Box 2, De la Rue House, Regent Street, London, W1) both offer attempts to synthesize judgements which have been solicited from former students of training courses; though these are inevitably subjective they would be worth consulting.

Introductory courses for training officers are offered by over thirty establishments of higher education. These courses are usually of a sandwich nature, involving a block of about four weeks in the college, followed by an individual project on the job, and then a final two or three weeks in the college. These courses are approved by the Department of Employment.

Part-time courses, diplomas. The City and Guilds Further Education Teachers' Certificates (see p. 203) are also appropriate to training officers.

The University of Manchester offers a one-year Diploma in Industrial Education Training on a full-time, sandwich or part-time basis. The University of Newcastle-upon-Tyne will shortly be offering a one-year course for the Diploma in Vocational Education and Industrial Training. Sheffield Polytechnic has a proposed modular course for the Certificate in Training Practice. Six-month courses for the Postgraduate Diploma in Industrial Training are offered by three colleges of technology – Hendon, Slough and Wolverhampton.

Resources

There are, perhaps, just a few remarkable and unusual teachers whose own stores of experiences are rich enough to sustain their classes without reference to books, films, television, transparencies, slides, tapes, or any of the other current aids to learning. Such teachers have always been rare, and the majority will always need at least some of these resources. Any teacher who has made even modest attempts to search for and prepare this type of material will know that it can often be time-consuming and frustrating. It requires money, organizational ability, management skills, persistence, ruthlessness and charm, otherwise it is likely to end in failure:

This is the story of how I tried to use a television programme for my class. I started by looking for the booking forms for the TV set, but someone had swiped them. I tracked them down after about two days and filled one in. A few days later I asked the visual aids technician if he had seen the booking. He looked surprised and said someone had swiped the book so he hadn't been bothering with the TV unless someone asked him on the day. Because of this, when the day came round, I took the precaution of arriving an hour early. I knocked on the door of the audio-visual aids room, but no one was there – supper break, union rules, etc. OK, I'd get the thing myself. Who had the key? No one knew. Unfortunately the one missing key on the board was the key to the a/v room and the man with the duplicate set locked his room in the evenings and took the key home with him. About ten minutes before the programme was due to start, the technician strolled up – don't panic, it's all planned. Unfortunately, he had a tape to copy so he couldn't carry it up the three flights of stairs for me, never mind, it's only a portable set. Breathless I arrived at the classroom – five minutes to go. A quick look round the room for the socket – in the worst possible place for watching TV – then disaster! It's the wrong type of socket for the plug on the set. A hardy young student raced down for a conversion extension. It took him a long time because the technician thought he might have loaned out all the right sort. However – success at last. We plugged in, switched on, the credits rolled, we settled down. I suppose we watched five minutes before the sound went, then the picture. Sorry lads, set's broken down. It turned out not to have been serviced for two years because servicing is 'expensive'.

Even at the planning stage, the decision to use a wide variety of resources can involve the tutor in an ever-spreading and complex network of telephone calls, visits, courses and personal contacts, all needing time, initiative and patience if they are to be followed up fully, as in this course which linked a TV series about a famous eighteenth-century house with local eighteenth-century history.

The television series was good for a term, but I didn't know enough about local history to cover a second term. I had been attending a course on how to get the source material of local history, but didn't have the time to search for it. At about the same time I had joined the newly formed local-history society and made the acquaintance of the borough archivist. She loaned me books on local history and suggested various maps and prints that would be of use. More important, she offered to have photostats made for me, an offer I jumped at. The institute had said that as this was a new course I could have a grant of £20 for materials.

The television series had indicated that the house was owned by the National Trust, so I contacted them to find out if there were any slides of that particular house. They put me in touch with the firm that made the slides and I bought an excellent selection.

A readers' guide issued by the Library Association listed all the books I would need on almost every subject connected with the period I intended to cover. In the end I decided that I couldn't read everything and instead of telling my future students what I had read, I would give them a reading list and they could find out for themselves.

Fashion was one of the things I wanted to cover. I went to Bath and visited the excellent costume museum – but there were no slides of costumes. Remembering that the Victoria and Albert Museum also had a large section on costume I rang them, to find out that there was a loan scheme and I could borrow their black-and-white slides.

I also wanted to use a tape recorder for playing some music of the period. There had been a radio programme about street ballads and I thought how splendid it would be if I could record some of them. Being a fairly lawful person I asked permission first, only to find out that one of the contributors to the programme demanded a fee for the use of his material for one occasion only and I thought it was too high, so decided against a tape recorder.

I am also going on a crash weekend course for research methods in local history and have contacted other members of the local-history society to see if they can lend me materials.

Added to the persistence and organizational skills needed to plan a course on this scale, a teacher wanting to use modern resources may find himself fighting a feeling among his bosses, his peers or his students that such resources are somehow frivolous or immoral. Hostility of this kind has a long tradition, and is still by no means dead:

Dr Fisher [then Archbishop of Canterbury] described television for schools as nothing less than a perfect disaster. It drove another wedge between the teacher and the pupil, and was bad for the children, who ought to be looking to the personal contribution of the teacher for their own personal growth. It was a dangerous thing when they thought they could be educated by mechanisms from outside (*The Times*, 7 March 1952).

So let's forget all the brainwashing which seeks to part teachers from their meagre requisition allowances in return for so much doubtful hardware. And let's look at those things which remain at the very core of education and which will do so for many years yet (J. C. Gagg, *Teacher's World*, 7 March 1970).

Nevertheless, many teachers would feel today that by themselves they cannot hope to be all things to all their students; they would have an uneasy feeling that the superiority of learning through print is no longer obvious to their students, particularly the younger ones, and that they must bring the world into the classroom, instead of attempting to shut it out by, in Marshall McLuhan's words, seeing education as 'civil defence against media fallout'.

No self-respecting training centre, evening institute or technical college would dream of being without a library, but how many of them also stock as a matter of course hundreds of tapes, 8-mm film loops, slides, records and films? Of the few who do hold such stocks, how many also have booths for individual listening or viewing? How many are filing articles and press cuttings on microfilm? How many have plans for computer terminals? A library able to offer such facilities is no longer simply a place where books are stored and catalogued, it has become a learning-resource centre of enormous potential.

Until such centres become commonplace there is hard work for the teacher who wishes to use a wide variety of resources, and no one could blame a poorly paid teacher if he refused to undertake the research involved in tracking them down. The trouble is not that there are too few resources, but there are too many, and that they are too widely diffused. Teachers and training officers can waste hours of time leafing through film catalogues, poring over bibliographies and library cards, or simply preparing home-made visual aids which might be obtained more cheaply and with less time and trouble from a professional source. When researching resources the secret of time-saving is a simple one; never try tracking down a film, a lecturer, a wallchart by yourself if there is some other person or organization whose job it is to do it.

In time this aspect of the search for materials should become extremely simple. Some wealthy universities have already installed systems where all the teacher or student has to do is to dial a number linking him with a computer, which will tell him in seconds what is available from the university's tape, slide, film and book collections. It would clearly be many hundred times more complex and expensive to develop a national system along the same lines, but the National Council for Educational Technology (160 Great Portland Street, London, W1) is already working on plans to provide a national multi-media data store. At first such a system would simply help the catalogue-producing agencies, or organizations which receive many requests for information, but in time immediate access to non-book resources by individual teachers should be a possibility.

In the meantime, the gap is filled by the invaluable work of the National Organization for Audio-Visual Aids, 33 Queen Anne Street, London, W1M OAL. This organization, financed by local education authorities, exists to give impartial technical advice on equipment, to train teachers, to research into audio-visual teaching methods, and to publish extensive catalogues of films, filmstrips, transparencies, wallcharts, 8-mm cassette loop films, and tapes prepared for educational use. The organization is the only one able to provide a single truly comprehensive source of information on audio-visual resources for education. Everything in the various catalogues can be viewed at the National Audio-Visual Aids Library, 2 Paxton Place, Gipsy Road, London, SE27. There are permanent large displays of equipment at the National Audio-Visual Aids Centre, 254/6 Belsize Road, London, NW6; the centre is always ready to receive personal queries by letter, telephone or visit. Journal: *Visual Education*, a monthly magazine with articles on equipment, practical use, reviews. One issue of this magazine is enlarged as a yearbook.

The secrets of successful *use* of resources are complex and have to do with the whole processes of teaching and learning. The teacher who cannot stand back and let a film do its work without constantly standing at his students' elbows interpreting, arguing, pushing his own point of view, is probably also too dominant in the rest of his class time. The teacher who continues to use only one textbook over many years is probably also the sort of teacher who never reassesses the rest of his teaching.

The only safe and simple rule that can be stated about using outside resources is that although using them may save the students time, and may make the learning strikingly more enjoyable, more vivid, more memorable, they inevitably involve the teacher in preparation time. Time must be allowed for setting up the tape-recorder; for writing to embassies, firms and local societies; for the occasions when equipment breaks down or the books fail to arrive. There must be planning and organization to cope with administration, recording and servicing.

Apart from that, there can only be the general rules of good educational practice to guide the teacher through the cornucopia of available resources.

Broadcasting

Broadcasting has obvious advantages – accessibility, cheapness, opportunities to bring the most expert of experts into the classroom, opportunities for stimulating interest with film, archive material or interviews on a scale which would be beyond the reach of most tutors. Added to this, both broadcasting authorities mount series with daytime and evening transmission times especially for adult classes. These could be short series concerned with leisure activities, with professional updating (for managers, teachers, doctors, supervisors), or thirty-programme courses in learning a language backed up by records, tapes, slides and teachers' notes. It is now legal to make sound and videotape recordings of all BBC and ITV educational programmes within certain not very constraining copyright limitations. Recording equipment is cheap, easy to operate, and means that teachers need not be bound to the often bizarre transmission times educational programmes are given. Programmes and series do not have to be used in their entirety – recording now makes it possible to use only the most useful highlights as and when the teacher chooses.

The class does not have to watch or listen as a group in class time. It may be more convenient to do this at home.

The most common mistake made by tutors making tape recordings of broadcasts is to put a microphone in front of the radio. A direct connection between radio and tape recorder will vastly improve the quality of the recording.

Details and advance information on school and further education series can be obtained from: BBC Further Education Liaison Office, Broadcasting House, Portland Place, London, W1A IAA, and The Education Officer, Independent Television Authority, 70 Brompton Road, London, SW3.

Celebrities

Celebrities, major and minor, local and national expert practitioners of whatever art the class has assembled to study, are often much more approachable than tutors think. Most creative-writing classes would benefit by a visit from a professional novelist or poet, most industrial-relations classes would enjoy a discussion with a well-known 'troubleshooter'. The rule usually is that the more eminent the person the more willing he is to undertake occasional visits of this kind, and the less likely he is to ask for a fee.

Closed-circuit television

Closed-circuit television offers a valuable learning aid to organizations which can afford it. CCTV systems are not usually worth installing unless they include at least two cameras with direct-vision viewfinders, several monitors and a videotape recorder. Amateurish television can irritate students, who are used to the impeccable professionalism of network broadcasting. It is vital, therefore, to have qualified staff to run the system, and to be clear about what it is possible for a small CCTV system to do well: simple interviews, case studies, discreet observation, demonstrations or details of processes too fine to be observed by large numbers of people by any other means.

Duplicating

Duplicating by spirit duplicators or stencils is cheap, but a plentiful supply of skilled secretarial help is essential, otherwise the untidy end product (handwritten or amateurishly typed) and long hours spent on preparation make it unprofitable. Even so, duplicated notes prepared and distributed in advance are one of the best ways of putting over large amounts of the more tedious information a class may need to have. There is no excuse today for the teacher who spends hours of precious class time with his back to the class furiously scribbling yards of notes which he expects the class to copy down. Photocopying methods have multiplied and improved enormously over the last ten years. Machines vary in efficiency, convenience in use, and cost, but photocopying is still the swiftest method of reproducing a small number of copies of a document, a newspaper article, a page of a book, and has the advantage of giving a realistic authentic touch to a folder of case-study documents or other discussion materials. Most training centres and evening institutes would have some kind of photocopying equipment, but may be reluctant to make large-scale use of it when the cost of each copy can be up to 10p. Some machines are sophisticated and can only be used by one trained operator, so advance booking may be essential.

Embassies and commercial organizations

Embassies and large commercial organizations often have public-relations and information departments which are useful sources of cheap or free demonstration material. Since such material is made for advertising purposes, it naturally praises the product. Nevertheless, many organizations provide excellent services to teachers. For instance, the Gas Council will lend working models of thermostats, magnetic boards for kitchen planning, free films, transparencies, and will advise on new equipment. Many firms, embassies or councils which promote particular commodities also run a speakers' service. The best collection of information and addresses is in the NUT Schoolmaster Publishing Company's *Treasure Chest for Teachers*. Inquiries to Derbyshire House, St Chad's Street, London, WC1.

Films

Films have a well-established place in the teacher's armoury even though film is comparatively fragile, needs expensive, heavy, well-maintained projection equipment and impeccable viewing facilities. The availability of cheap 8-mm cameras makes tailor-made instructional film a real possibility now, but most teachers would still find themselves needing to hire from the main distributors of 16-mm films. Many hundreds of films can be hired free; for others there is a charge, often at reduced rates for educational showings. There are well over sixty organizations which make or distribute films for hire. Some of the most useful catalogues can be obtained from:

Central Film Library
Government Buildings
Bromyard Avenue
Acton, London, W3

Common Ground (1951) Ltd
44 Fulham Road
London, SW3

Concordia Films and Publishing House Ltd
Concordia House
117–23 Golden Lane
London, EC1

Connoisseur Films Ltd
54–8 Wardour Street
London, W1

Gateway Educational Films Ltd
470 Green Lanes
London, N13

Rank Film Library
1 Aintree Road
Perivale
Greenford, Middlesex

Sound Services Ltd
Kingston Road
Merton Park
London, SW19

Some films become educational classics and are frequently bought by local education authorities and training centres for free loan to teachers. It is always worth inquiring about LEA film stocks.

For any film show it is essential to book well in advance – some films are so popular that they are booked a year ahead.

Film loops

Film loops are 8-mm films sealed in casettes which can be slotted into a special projector incorporating a daylight-viewing screen. They are useful for the kind of industrial or scientific process which students might want to watch in slow or accelerated motion, or for demonstration sequences which benefit from being seen over and over again, individually or in groups. A catalogue of film-loop casettes is available from the National Organization for Audio-Visual Aids. The main drawback at present to this promising resource is that the choice of material is much more limited than it is for films.

Filmstrips and slides

It would be hard to think of a classroom subject which could not be made more graphic by the use of filmstrips and slides. Stocks of commercially made products are cheap enough to buy and are easily added to by the teacher's own photography. Synchronized tape-slide presentations can also be home-made; it is always worth watching out for BBC educational radiovision programmes, where the teacher buys a filmstrip or set of slides in advance and then tapes the broadcast for replay later. Many filmstrips can be borrowed free; hire charges are modest on commercially distributed filmstrips.

Libraries

The local library is still the tutor's best friend as far as printed material goes. Most county and borough librarians offer special services to adult education and will go to considerable trouble to obtain what the teacher wants. Here are some examples of what libraries can do :

1. Lend sets of plays, music scores, gramophone records on long loan from special collections.
2. Assemble groups of books for a padlocked 'book box' which is delivered direct to the classroom.
3. Arrange for the teacher to receive rare books from specialist libraries in other parts of the country.
4. Offer research facilities from their own archives for students and teachers.

5. Make photocopies, sets or singles at reasonable charge of documents, magazine articles, single pages in rare books, or reference works which cannot be lent out.

Of all the library services the most valuable element in them is the librarian himself who, by showing a teacher the way round bibliographies, catalogues and indexes, can save an inexperienced teacher hours of wasteful dithering.

Local societies

Local societies are one of the best potential sources of help. For instance, a local-history society may have built up priceless collections of documents which it is willing to lend or have copied; a local conservation group, ramblers' club or ornithological society should be a useful place to find specialist lecturers; photographic clubs and film societies may be willing to make free or cost-price visual aids; a consumer group may have information from surveys of local food and prices. Libraries are the places to find out names and secretaries' addresses.

Museums and art galleries

Museums and art galleries take some trouble with their education services, though these are not nearly as fully used as they might be by teachers of adults. Most museums can offer:

1. Rooms where groups can work on projects, objects from special collections which students can touch and inspect closely at their leisure.
2. A loan scheme where objects, documents and working models can be delivered direct to a class.
3. Collections of photostated documents of local and national interest.
4. A lecturer service.
5. Collections of slides and filmstrips for free loan.

It will be obvious to historians that it is valuable to have opportunities to handle objects from the past. What is not so obvious is that a pottery class might relish the opportunities to examine at close quarters the local museum's stock of Samian ware, or Chinese porcelain; a class in ornithology might use a museum's natural-history section to work on specimens which represent unique local collections of birds; a dressmaking or embroidery class might find special interest in working out the techniques used on costumes or fragments of embroidery from the past.

Societies and associations

National societies and associations are an excellent first place for teachers of particular subjects to search for information and advice. Some exist to encourage greater professionalism among members or to be the spearhead of new teaching methods – e.g. the National Association for the Teaching of English, the Mathematical Association, the Historical Association. Others, like the Consumers Association, Oxfam, the National Trust, the English Folk Dance and Song Society exist as pressure groups or clubs which take their educational duties seriously and can offer substantial teaching materials, often free or at very low cost. Most such organizations have small but highly specialized libraries.

A good collection of names and addresses of national societies and associations is assembled in *Treasure Chest for Teachers* (see p. 211).

Other institutions

Other institutions may have equipment and resources which they are willing to share. Here are some possibilities:

1. Local art colleges are usually happy to prepare printed material, wallcharts, display stands.
2. Another centre may be willing to build up a joint slide and tape collection.
3. There may be parallel classes in other institutes which could be occasionally combined for one-day schools, evening conferences, or visits.

Colleagues

Other teachers have other skills which it is often profitable to utilize in a team-teaching arrangement, by which classes combine for a lecture, demonstration or exhibition in between work in much smaller groups. By this sensible system the specialisms of different teachers can be fully exploited, but the flexibility achieved needs organization and strong nerves to carry through successfully.

Overhead projectors

The overhead projector looks set fair to rival the blackboard as the most useful and versatile visual aid. It can be used in daylight, is extremely simple to operate, and a teacher can write on the rolls of blank re-usable acetate film without turning his back on the class. Simple photocopying produces cheap and vivid transparencies made from pages of books, charts or maps which have excellent definition and can be seen easily by everyone. A series of transparencies can be made as 'overlays' where, for instance complex diagrams and charts can be built up. Working diagrams are easily made with hinged pieces of perspex and balsa wood. Books for the teacher's classroom use are now being prepared by the Pergamon Press with ingenious flip-over transparencies, and no doubt stocks of printed transparencies will go on increasing rapidly.

Programmed texts

Programmed texts are being produced in ever-increasing quantities. An elaborate compilation of programmes in print is published in the *Yearbook of Educational and Instructional Technology*, published by Cornmarket Press for the Association for Programmed Learning and Educational Technology, 27 Torrington Square, London, WC1. The same yearbook contains information on language laboratories and teaching machines.

Tape

Tape is vital to language teachers, both for providing plentiful practice in listening to speech and to enable students to listen to and record their own efforts. It is a useful resource also for teachers of drama, speech, sociology, physical education, literature and history, either as a way of recording work done, or as a way of storing aural information. Many educational publishers are now offering tapes with books and teachers' notes as complete 'learning packages'.

A catalogue of *Recorded Sound for Education* is available from the National Organization for Audio-Visual Aids.

Schools Council

The Schools Council is basically an organization concerned with school examinations and curricula. Even so, its development projects are not only research bodies but also produce packages of materials for classroom use, many of which could be used as flexibly and interestingly for adult classes as they can for schools. Even the projects concerned with the education of young children (such as the Leeds University Project for Teaching English to Immigrant Children) may suggest methods and materials which could be easily adapted for adults.

Of more direct interest to adult classes might be the projects concerned with the humanities, moral education, technology, German, Spanish and Russian, secondary mathematics and secondary science, linguistics and English teaching. Addresses from 160 Great Portland Street, London, W1.

Index

Index

Other Penguin Education Specials

Resources for Learning

L. C. Taylor

From all sides the traditional methods of classroom teaching are under pressure. They encourage passivity. They cannot easily cope with the range of abilities and interests found in most classes. They make hopelessly inefficient use of an already understaffed teaching force. In an education system which increasingly values individual learning, they are dangerously inflexible.

In this penetrating and highly original book, L. C. Taylor shows how the methods of education are inextricably related to the purpose we ascribe to it. If, for instance, we want a comprehensive system where children of different abilities learn together, then we must be prepared to devise new techniques to achieve this.

Drawing on his experience previously as headmaster of Sevenoaks School and now as Director of the Nuffield Resources for Learning Project, and also his researches in Russia, America and Sweden, L. C. Taylor examines critically the new techniques and instruments of classroom modernization, from individualized learning and team teaching, to computer-assisted instruction and closed-circuit television.

Teaching and Learning in Higher Education

Ruth Beard

Provision for higher education is now recognized as a major social and educational need. In the United Kingdom alone, a million students by 1980 is no longer a wild statistic, but a realistic basis for forward planning. At the start of a new decade of expansion, Ruth Beard has produced a timely and comprehensive analysis of the nature of teaching and learning in higher education.

Drawing on innovations in teaching methods in universities and colleges, as well as on findings from educational research, Dr Beard examines ways in which the current upsurge of new ideas is affecting curricula, courses and teaching techniques. After a chapter on different psychological approaches to human learning, which sets out the theoretical background to the practical problems under discussion, the middle chapters of the book provide a rigorous analysis of the educational value of the lecture, the seminar, laboratory and small-group teaching.

The author, believing that courses cannot be fully effective unless teachers reconsider their methods in relation to their aims and objectives, evaluates important preliminary research which has looked at the interaction between teacher and student in different learning situations.

Teaching and Learning in Higher Education demonstrates the vital need to ensure further improvements in the quality of teaching during the coming years. The book will be of particular value to teachers in universities and colleges, and also to those who are likely to benefit most from the raising of standards – the students themselves.